HOW TO MAI

C000173370

In this Series

Other titles in preparation

MANAGE AN
OFFICE

Planning and creating a successful workplace

Ann Dobson

SORRY, JIM, I'VE FOUND
SOMEONE TO REPLACE
YOU!

How To Books

Other books by the same author

How to Return to Work
How to Manage Meetings
How to Write Business Letters

Cartoons by Mike Flanagan

British Library Cataloguing in Publication Data
A catalogue record for this book is available from the British Library.

First published in 1995 by How To Books Ltd, Plymbridge House, Estover Road, Plymouth PL6 7PZ, United Kingdom. Tel: (01752) 735251/695745. Fax: (01752) 695699. Telex: 45635.

Note: The material contained in this book is set out in good faith for general guidance and no liability can be accepted for loss or expense incurred as a result of relying in particular circumstances on statements made in this book. The laws and regulations may be complex and liable to change, and readers should check the current position with the relevant authorities before making personal arrangements.

Typeset by Concept Communications (Design & Print) Ltd, Crayford, Kent. Printed and bound by The Cromwell Press, Broughton Gifford, Melksham, Wiltshire

Contents

List of Illustrations

IS THIS YOU?

Manager   Employment consultant

Health trust executive

Estate agent   Haulage contractor

Partner

Counsellor   Retailer

Designer

Optician   Wine merchant

Farmer

Travel agent   Architect

Caterer

Wholesaler   Sports promoter

Solicitor

Self-employed   Auctioneer

Consultant

Surveyor   Club secretary

Secretary

Hotel manager   Manufacturer

Antique dealer

Personal assistant   Literary agent

Accountant

Car dealer   Head teacher

Veterinary surgeon

Dentist   Insurance agent

PR consultant

Mortgage broker   Doctor

Kennel owner

Party planner   Financial adviser

Funeral director

Preface

The office world is changing rapidly. Almost every business task today can be performed by means of technology. At the same time it is very important for those in charge of managing offices to show that they can still function like caring, innovative human beings rather than impersonal machines.

How to Manage an Office offers a completely new insight into the office of today and of the future. Whether you work for yourself or someone else, are about the set up an office, or already work in one, by the time you finish this book you will be well equipped to face any challenges, technological or otherwise, that lie ahead. In fact, *How to Manage an Office* will interest anyone who intends to be involved with the office world of today or tomorrow, even if you are still at school or college.

Throughout the book four case studies are used to illustrate various office situations. Read in conjunction with the relevant chapters, these case studies add real life interest, and often humour, to lighten the facts explained in the text.

We live in an exciting 'new age' and nowhere is this more noticeable than in our working lives. *How to Manage an Office* aims to eliminate any fears you may have about your ability to change and adapt as technology develops still further.

Ann Dobson

1
The Office:
Past, Present and Future

In this first chapter we will:

- step back in time
- trace the development of the modern office
- understand the different kinds of organisation
- think about the functions of any office
- consider the changes taking place
- decide where you fit in
- discuss working in the office of the future.

STEPPING BACK IN TIME

The office world of today is far removed from the Dickensian image of the male clerk sitting on a high stool at a high desk using a quill pen to write a laborious manuscript. In those days there was hardly a machine or a woman in sight, unlike now where there are usually more machines than people and more women than men in our typical 'hi tech' office.

In fact the male clerk dates back to the 13th century. At that time, and until the mid to late 19th century, they were considered to be high up members of society, almost on the same level as professional men. Employed to copy manuscript, write letters and do bookkeeping, they reigned supreme in the office world until women and machinery came along to change their way of life for ever.

Unfortunately for the men, women were found to be better at operating the new business machinery introduced in the late 1800s. They were also cheaper to employ and made far less fuss about their working conditions and status in life.

In the 1870s the first commercially produced typewriter was introduced. It was known as the Sholes-Glidden machine. The women operating the early typewriters were known as 'typewriters' and their machines were called 'type writers'.

Very early offices were often in the homes of merchants or in coffee houses. From the 1700s onwards more offices began to move into commercial premises of various kinds. During the 1800s, offices began to be more departmentalised, and gradually developed in size and complexity to accommodate the growing number of men and women employed in them.

TRACING THE DEVELOPMENT OF THE MODERN OFFICE

By the beginning of the 20th century, the telephone, the typewriter, the duplicator and electricity were all evident in the office.

Let us take a brief look at the chronological developments:

- 1830s — Railways took over from the stage coach for delivery of letters. Isaac Pitman published the first edition of his shorthand system.

- 1840s — Penny Post introduced.

- 1870s — First commercial typewriters produced. Telephone invented by Alexander Bell.

- 1880s — Stencil duplicating started by David Gestetner. First dictating machines introduced. Electric light bulbs began to replace gas lamps.

- 1920s — Postage meters and franking machines introduced.

- 1940s — First electronic computer called ENIAC was built in the USA.

Early offices bore very little resemblance to what we know as an office today. Even as late as between the two world wars, they were still shabby, miserable places in which to work.

During the second world war (1939-45) many city centres were destroyed and this gave the planners the chance to design new offices that really did cater for the people working in them. Specialised office blocks were constructed, unfortunately many of them in skyscraper buildings which destroyed the surrounding landscape. As far as the planners were concerned, however, many more people could be fitted into, for instance, a 12-floor office block than a double-storey building.

The 1963 Offices, Shops and Railways Act laid down minimum requirements for the welfare and safety of, amongst others, office workers. These requirements were, in most cases, well met anyway by the new office blocks, but at least office workers now knew that they would all be working in satisfactory conditions.

Over the last 50 years offices have gradually become more comfortable and pleasant places in which to work. The male orientated environment has largely disappeared and men and women work alongside one another, perhaps not always in harmony, but at least respecting each other's status in the office hierarchy.

HOW DIFFERENT ORGANISATIONS WORK

There are many different kinds of organisations, both in the **private sector** and the **public sector**.

Private sector
The sole trader
Although a sole trader can be a shopkeeper, an innkeeper, a hairdresser or employed in many other occupations, for our purposes, we shall think of a sole trader as someone who owns and runs their own organisation involving an office or offices. This person is classed as being self-employed and is liable for any debts that are incurred in the business.

The partnership
This is a similar organisation to that of the sole trader, but in this case two or more (up to 20) people own the business and they are all self-employed. Usually, like the sole trader, the partners are liable for any debts.

The private limited liability company
In a private limited liability company, the owners put money in by buying shares in that company. If the company then incurs debts each shareholder is liable up to the value of his or her investment. Private limited liability companies have Ltd or Limited after their name.

The public limited liability company
These companies sell their shares to the general public. This is usually, although not always, done through the Stock Exchange. A public limited liability company is governed by a board of directors. The company has plc after its name.

Public sector

Public sector organisations include central government departments, local government departments, The Bank of England, and nationalised industries. They are all state owned.

THINKING ABOUT THE FUNCTIONS OF ANY OFFICE

The functions and activities of any office are many and diverse. They all, however, hinge around two key words: **information** and **communication**.

Information is:

- received
- obtained
- sorted
- arranged
- interpreted
- sent out
- stored
- retrieved.

For successful information handling, we use a variety of mechanical, electronic and manual systems.

The definition of the word communication is to give, receive or exchange information.

Effective office communication is achieved by:

- speaking face to face
- speaking on the telephone
- listening to others
- observing the body language of others
- letters, memos, faxes and messages
- computer link-up.

If information is handled in an appropriate way, by using effective communication methods, then the office will function successfully. On the other hand, in a badly run office, where everyone fails to communicate effectively, valuable information, time, and business will be lost.

CONSIDERING THE CHANGES TAKING PLACE

If you pick up an office skills textbook written ten years ago, you will immediately see how things have changed even in such a relatively short period of time. A book written 20 years ago will have little or no relevance to today's office. Whether we like it or not we are living in a technological age, an age where we are having to get used to working with machines of every shape, size and purpose, both in the office and at home.

During the last 20 years we have seen the computer develop to such an extent that virtually every office uses at least one, and many offices have networks of machines all linked to a central base. Computerised accounts can be prepared, charts and diagrams can be produced in seconds, and files holding masses of information can be stored on disk.

Secretaries who, 20 years ago, plugged away on a manual typewriter, or maybe an electric machine, now use a word processing package and a computer to produce their everyday letters. They can edit the letter, correct it, and only print out the final copy when they are completely happy with the result. Another nightmare in the secretary's life, carbon paper for copies of correspondence, has almost become a thing of the past. Either two copies can be printed out by the computer printer, or else a photocopy can be taken.

Faxed messages, letters, and other documents can be sent from one office to another in seconds. Telephones have been improved dramatically, and very soon videophones, where we can look at the person as we speak to them, will, no doubt, be widely in use.

The actual technicalities of much of the above will be discussed in more detail in Chapter 8, but suffice to say that changes are taking place at a very rapid rate. Unfortunately, the downside of the technological age is that as the number of technological aids grow, the number of staff needed, in general, decreases.

DECIDING WHERE YOU FIT IN

If you are going to manage any kind of office, you will need to make sure you have the appropriate skills and qualifications for the job. This will not necessarily mean gaining formal qualifications, particularly if you are working for yourself, but you should be capable of carrying out all the necessary duties efficiently.

A machine is only as good as its operator, and so far as using modern electronic equipment is concerned, it will be up to you to prove both to yourself and to your staff, that you can all work alongside these new aids, rather than be afraid of them. Machines do not have a mind of their

ARE YOU:

- positive
- conscientious
- reliable
- loyal
- organised
- unflappable
- polite
- well-groomed
- diplomatic
- sympathetic
- helpful

- dedicated
- hard working
- approachable
- cheerful
- experienced
- tactful
- smart
- firm
- efficient
- friendly
- tough-skinned

DO YOU:

- show initiative
- set an example
- listen
- achieve
- delegate

- establish a good rapport
- motivate people
- communicate effectively
- work well under pressure
- possess the relevant skills

Fig. 1. The questions to ask **before** managing an office.

own (although it may seem so at times!) and adequate training should provide you and your staff with the confidence to treat these machines as friends rather than enemies. Many older people, in particular, have an inbuilt hatred of anything new and it is up to you to overcome their prejudices.

As far as personal qualities are concerned, the most important ones are shown in Figure 1. It is very important that you are able to motivate and support any staff you may be managing. If you look and act in a negative way, they will do the same. Conversely, if you can show a positive and dedicated attitude in all you do, they are far more likely to respond in a similar way.

WORKING IN THE OFFICE OF THE FUTURE

None of us knows exactly what the future has in store. Perhaps that is just as well. But one thing is sure: the office, in one form or another, will be around for a very long time to come.

It is said by many that traditional large office buildings as such will become more and more of a rarity in future. This is because:

● an increasing number of people will be running their own business, either from home or from smaller office premises.

● more employees will be home based, using various electronic aids to link up with their head office. This gives the advantage to an employee of not having to spend time travelling to work, and to an employer of saving expensive office costs.

● companies may increase the use of 'hot desking' which means that more than one person shares each office desk. This works well when employees are either home based or travel around the country, and again saves valuable office space.

● large organisations are, in many cases, getting smaller.

It has to be said that it is unlikely that there will ever again be the job security that used to exist within large, 'dependable' organisations. No job is safe any more, and the trend amongst more and more businesses is to employ their staff on a part-time or contract basis.

The gradual decline in the number of large organisations, coupled with the increase in smaller organisations, means that more people than ever before will be involved in managing their own or an employer's office. The following chapters will explain how this important task can best be tackled.

CHECKLIST

● Do you possess the relevant experience and skills to manage an office?

● If not, are you prepared to acquire them?

● Are you familiar with the different kinds of organisations?

● What are the functions of an office?

● Are you prepared for the changing office environment?

● Can you visualise the office of the future?

INTRODUCTION TO CASE STUDIES

Throughout the book several cases studies will be used to illustrate the various points made in each chapter. The main four that we will follow are:

Dorothy the school secretary

Dorothy is aged 50 and is a real fusspot. She works as a school secretary in a small, private prep school. A new headmistress has recently been appointed who is young, dynamic and go-ahead. She wants Dorothy to bring the office up to date. Dorothy has not got a clue where to start. She has two, equally old fashioned, part-timers working under her.

Sue plans to work from home

Sue is a 35 year old modern mum, about to set up her own employment agency. She loves all the new technology and intends to make full use of it in her office. As she has a very large house she intends to work from home. She will not have any staff working in the office, just her 'temp' ladies to employ.

Stephen is promoted

Stephen, who is 28, has been working for a very large estate agency in

London. He is fed up with commuting and has asked for a transfer to his local office. Fortunately for him, a manager's vacancy has arisen and Stephen is offered this position. He will be going from a dynamic London office to a much smaller and slower paced environment. He wants to expand and update this new office, but he is taking over from someone who was very popular with the staff and clients, so he will have to tread carefully.

John the hospital administrator

John is a 45 year old hospital administrator. The hospital he works for has just been awarded trust status and John has been asked to take over the administration of the outpatient department. Due to an increase in demand, the outpatient department is to be moved to another part of the hospital. This means that John is taking on a new job and then arranging an office move, all in a very short space of time.

POINTS FOR DISCUSSION

1. What would you say to a member of your staff who refused to attend a computer training course?

2. Do you think the office of the future will offer more or less job security?

3. Do you think women and men are treated equally in the modern office? Give reasons for your answer.

2
Setting Up a New Office

If you are intending to set up a completely new office, a good deal of planning and preparation will need to take place beforehand.

In this chapter we will discuss:

- researching your market
- working from home
- finding outside premises
- arranging finance
- checking on planning permission
- thinking about car parking
- deciding decor and layout
- choosing office hardware
- advertising your goods/services.

RESEARCHING YOUR MARKET

Whatever type of office you intend to set up and manage, a considerable amount of research should be undertaken to make sure that your business idea is a sound one.

Business ideas fall into two main categories:

- those that build on other people's concepts

- entirely new concepts — that is, where no one else has tried the particular business idea you envisage.

In general, it is better to play safe and build on other people's concepts. It might just be that you have a revolutionary idea that will take off and earn you millions of pounds, but the reality is that if an idea has not been tried, maybe there is no market for it. On the other hand, never be afraid of some healthy competition. At least that means there is a market for your idea, just so long as you do it better than your competitors.

The main aim of your research is therefore to show that a market exists for your product or service and also to make sure that the market has not been saturated by too much competition.

The type of research you carry out will depend on the business you intend to start. Take a look at figure 2 for an illustration of this.

WORKING FROM HOME

Working from home has very definite advantages and disadvantages. Perhaps the two main reasons why people decide to run their business from home rather than from an outside office are:

● for financial reasons

● due to family commitments.

It is usually far cheaper to work from home rather than rent or buy an office somewhere else. Not only will you save the rent/loan repayments, but you will also save on travelling expenses to and from work. As far as family commitments are concerned, if you are working from home you are much more likely to be able to juggle looking after children or dependent elderly relatives.

Other advantages in working from home

● Home is more convenient.

● You can work erratic hours.

● Generally speaking, home is more comfortable.

● You can work a longer day without travelling times.

● You are 'on the spot' at all times to deal with any problems that arise in either your working or home life.

Disadvantages in working from home

● Work can interfere with home life.

● The temptation may be to keep working with no break.

Situation: Mark Adams wants to set up an office and factory producing and selling double glazed windows and doors. What does he need to research?

1. The competition he is up against:
   He can do this by looking in *Yellow Pages* and local papers and then visiting several competitors pretending to be an interested customer.

2. How much money he will need:
   An accountant will help him to prepare a business plan and assess whether Mark has the right financial base on which to start his business.

3. The chance he stands of succeeding:
   This depends on whether there really is a gap in the market that Mark can fill.

4. Suitable premises for his new venture:
   Mark wants a large office suitable for himself and some telesales staff. He also needs a small factory where the products can be assembled.

5. Availability of suitable staff:
   As the business is not just dependent on him, Mark will want to recruit staff who will be dedicated enough to help him to get his new business off the ground.

6. Availability of suitable suppliers:
   Mark has to find suitable suppliers for all his raw materials.

Only after all this research has been carried out can Mark really know whether or not he is wise to go ahead.

Fig. 2. The importance of effective research.

- Conversely, it can be tempting not to 'go to work'. Gardening or watching television might seem more attractive.

- Your home may not have sufficient accommodation.

- You may not be able to get permission from the council and/or your mortgage lender to run a business from home.

- Your property deeds may prohibit the running of a business.

- Your home may not be in a suitable location, *ie* out in the country.

Should you be about to embark on any business venture it is worth taking the time and trouble to investigate working from home, as this can certainly save you a considerable amount of money, particularly during the first couple of years.

FINDING OUTSIDE PREMISES

If, for one reason or another, you have decided that your home is not suitable for your business venture, then you will have to find premises elsewhere. This will involve checking the newspaper and also contacting agents who deal in commercial property. Assuming you can afford to rent or buy, look into both options before making up your mind.

Points to remember when buying a property

- Negotiate a good **price** for the premises. No sensible owner expects to be paid the asking price.

- Have a **survey** carried out to make sure the premises are in good condition. If there are problems then re-negotiate the price.

- If you need to borrow the money to buy the premises make sure that you are able to obtain the necessary **finance**.

- Check on the terms of the **lease** if the property is leasehold rather than freehold.

- Check out the business **rates**.

Points to remember when renting a property

● Make sure that you will be paying a fair **rent**. Negotiate if necessary.

● Ask what is included in the rent, *ie* heating, lighting etc.

● Check on whether you have to pay your own business **rates**. If so, find out how much they are.

● Find out how much **notice** you will need to offer should you decide to give up the premises.

● Check what **obligations** you have in the way of re-decoration, maintenance etc.

It is very important to cost out **everything** involved when either buying or renting premises. And don't forget: you will need money for re-decorating and perhaps improvements too.

ARRANGING FINANCE

How much finance you will need for your new office depends on the type of business you envisage. Many home-based businesses require very little capital to set up. On the other hand, a large business involving the renting or buying of large, up-market premises and the hiring of several staff will need a large cash injection.

It is possible, in certain circumstances, to join the Government's Business Start Up Scheme, whereby you will receive a small weekly cash payment for a limited amount of time, but this will not actually help you to set up the business.

If you do not have your own funds available, you will probably have to take out a loan of some kind. This could be in the form of a re-mortgage on your house, or else a business loan from one of the high street banks.

You should think very carefully before taking on any loan. Never overstretch yourself. Loan repayments at hefty rates of interest can cripple a business, particularly a new business without any reserves. Always remember that you have to be able to survive the first six months, perhaps a year or even two years, before profits start to come in from even the most successful business. A good accountant or bank manager should be able to advise you on how much you can safely borrow.

A bank will normally require a business plan. You can either prepare this yourself or enlist the help of an accountant. A business plan should show:

- what you intend to do
- where you intend to do it
- how much you would like to borrow
- why you think your idea is a good one
- your current financial position
- a forecast of money expected to come in during a given period.

CHECKING ON PLANNING PERMISSION

Whether you intend to work from home or from an outside office, you should check with the planning department of your local district council about planning permission and/or change of use. Office premises in office blocks will not normally require any permissions, but if, for instance, you intend to change a shop property into an office, you will need to apply for change of use. As far as a home office is concerned, it may be necessary to obtain planning permission if part of your home is to be permanently changed to business use.

Never go ahead and set up a new business without checking all this out first, otherwise your business could be forced to close. The rules for planning permission are very complicated and your local planning department will be able to tell you all the 'ins and outs' straight away, to save you making a mistake you could well regret.

Many people get very uptight about planning permission, where their home is concerned, saying that it is up to them to make any changes they wish to their own property, but the planning laws have to be adhered to, both in home and business life, and failure to do so can result in a disastrous situation arising after the business is up and running.

THINKING ABOUT CAR PARKING

Not all offices need car parking facilities. This applies to home-based businesses in particular, where nearly all the day-to-day communication is carried out by letter, fax and on the telephone, rather than by meeting people face to face. If, however, frequent visits are to be made to your office by clients, or you employ members of staff, then some serious consideration should be given to car parking.

Public car parks can be very expensive to use on a long term basis, as you will discover if you have to park your own car in one every day. It should be said, therefore, that if your type of business is reliant on car parking facilities, it is worth spending a good deal of time finding the right premises or house, rather than taking something unsuitable and then regretting it later.

DECIDING LAYOUT AND DECOR

Your budget will dictate, to a certain extent, how much style and panache you can give to your new office. Even on a limited budget, however, it is possible to create a pleasant, comfortable and practical working environment, if you give sufficient planning and forethought to what you want to achieve.

The layout of each office is the first important consideration. The traditional type is known as a **cellular** office. This is a normal room with doors and windows and it gives a good degree of privacy and peace to whoever works inside. A cellular office can accommodate one person or a small number of people.

A more modern idea is to create an **open plan** office. This is a large room divided up into sections, with or without screens to partition each area. Open plan offices, depending on their size, can house many people, all working in their own little sections. Staff working in an open plan office can liaise more freely with their colleagues, and many more can be accommodated in one large office than say two smaller ones. The big disadvantages of open plan offices, however, are firstly the noise level that staff have to endure, and secondly the lack of privacy.

The points to consider are:

- How many people will be working in the office?

- Will one small office, a group of offices, or an open plan office best suit your needs?

- What furniture and specialist equipment are necessary?

- How can that furniture and equipment be arranged to give maximum space and light?

- Have you considered the legal requirements as laid down in the Offices, Shops and Railway Premises Act, 1963, the Health and Safety at Work Act of 1974 and its later addition, the Management of Health and Safety at Work Regulations 1992? (See Chapter 13 for more details.)

In today's electronic office much of the planning is centred around the siting of computers and the necessary cables for the various pieces of equipment. Suffice it to say that everything should be arranged in such a way as to make working conditions as safe and comfortable as possible.

Everyone has their own idea on how to decorate their office. Generally speaking, pastel shades are thought to be best. Black or brown walls with a red carpet will not do much to encourage positive thinking! On the other hand, a few well chosen pictures, some decorative plants and attractive non-obtrusive pastel wall and carpet colouring will create an attractive place in which to work.

CHOOSING OFFICE HARDWARE

Within each office, the actual choice of desks, chairs and other furniture and equipment depends on your particular requirements. Never skimp on the important items such as the type of computer/s, the software necessary, the quality of fax machine etc. Conversely, do not spend any more money than is really necessary at the beginning. A few, well chosen, good quality pieces of equipment can always be added to later on.

Even though it may cost a little more money, purpose designed office furniture should be chosen for your new office, rather than cheap imitations. If you are on a limited budget you might like to consider buying some of the furniture secondhand. That way you will be able to get good quality at a lower price.

Care needs to be taken to see that chairs are the correct height for the desks, otherwise backache and other problems will occur.

Most offices contain the following:

- desks
- chairs of varying types for the workers plus seating for guests
- filing cabinets (to use as well as or instead of computer/microfilm storage facility)
- stationery cupboard or drawers
- personal computers and/or word processors and/or typewriters
- dot matrix, inkjet or laser printers
- fax machines
- telephones

- photocopier
- fire extinguishers
- reference books.

There are many other items of furniture and equipment that could be added to this list, but these are usually considered the essentials.

A good computer supplier should be able to give you helpful advice on exactly what makes and models would best suit your needs as far as the electronic equipment is concerned. They will also advise on the pros and cons of leasing rather than buying the equipment.

Be especially careful when choosing computer equipment. The memory needed to run many of the sophisticated software programs is increasing all the time, so you should always go for a machine with a bigger memory than you think you need.

ADVERTISING YOUR GOODS/SERVICES

A major reason why many businesses fail is a lack of advertising. If no one knows you exist then no one can do business with you. When setting up a new office it is therefore important to advertise your goods or services well in advance of starting up.

Advertising can take the form of newspaper advertisements and special reports, local radio broadcasts, leaflet drops, cards in shop windows, letters to companies/individuals, in fact any method that helps to spread the word about your new venture.

The example in figure 3 illustrates how effective advertising can make the difference between success and failure in today's competitive markets.

CHECKLIST

- Have you taken the time to research your chosen market?

- Are you aware of the competition?

- Are you going to work from home?

- If not, do you know of any suitable premises?

- Can you raise the necessary finance?

- Have you prepared a sound business plan?

- Do you need to apply for planning permission?

- Have you thought about car parking?

- Do you know how to design, equip and decorate your office?

- Are you aware of health and safety restrictions?

- Have you prepared a good advertising campaign?

CASE STUDY

Sue sets up her office

Sue wants to use two rooms of her house for her employment agency. She first of all checks her mortgage deeds to see whether there is a restriction on running a business. She then applies to the local council for planning permission and this is granted. She also arranges additional insurance cover to cater for the running of her business. As her house is detached and in its own grounds, there is parking for as many cars as she will ever need, without disturbing anyone else.

Sue sets about equipping her office rooms. She equips one as a reception office, where her temps can come in and sit in comfort while they are waiting to see her. Easy chairs, a big round central table, a coffee making machine and lots of appealing pictures on the walls, all add a welcoming touch.

One corner of the reception is partitioned off and a personal computer and printer, together with audio equipment, are installed. This she intends to use for cross-training on different software programs and for testing each of her prospective temps. They will type out a letter for her from written copy and using a dictaphone machine. If appropriate, she will then give them a shorthand test from a pre-recorded tape.

She equips her own office with another personal computer and printer, telephone, fax machine, and photocopier. For furniture she chooses a very large oak desk with deep drawers suitable for keeping all her records. Her winged chair is fully adjustable and well padded, ideal for sitting in for long periods of time as she expects to do. Along one wall she hangs portraits of her children to add a homely touch. The other walls are lined with the Lowry prints she has collected over a number of years.

Sue's next step is to write to all the companies she can come across within a ten mile radius of her home. She tells them about the new

Situation: Mark Adams (see figure 2) is going ahead with his business venture to manufacture and sell double glazed products. What advertising does he do to promote his business?

1. *Newspaper advertising*
   Mark uses display ads in the local newspapers to tell as many people as possible about his new business.

2. *Local radio advertising*
   He arranges a short ad, twice a day for a couple of weeks, to spread the message even further.

3. *Leaflet drops*
   Mark and perhaps a couple of his telesales staff cover the local area delivering leaflets describing the new company's products and incorporating a tear-off slip so that interested householders can contact him.

4. *Telesales advertising*
   Mark's telesales staff canvas as many households as possible.

5. *Personal recommendation*
   Mark gets known in the area, and he gradually begins to receive personal recommendation from satisfied customers.

6. *Sign advertising*
   Mark has signs erected outside his premises (after obtaining planning permission) to say who and what they are. He also has an advertisement put on the side of his car, for when he is out on the road.

Mark has the necessary finance, has carried out his research and advertising well and builds a successful business.

Fig. 3. Effective advertising.

agency and asks to make an appointment to visit them. She mentions very good opening rates to 'tempt' them away from their present agencies.

As far as advertising is concerned, Sue decides to advertise in the local papers only to start with. She feels that her most successful approach is to the companies direct and that the newspaper ads will just provide backup.

POINTS FOR DISCUSSION

1. 'Extensive research and advertising coupled with sufficient working capital spell success for any business venture.' How true do you consider this statement to be?

2. List all the advantages and disadvantages of working from home that you can think of.

3. Do you think that Sue (see Case Studies) could manage with just one rather than two personal computers in her office? Give reasons for your answer.

3
Recruiting Office Staff

Whether you are setting up your own business or managing an office for someone else, the chances are that at some time you will be involved with the recruiting of staff.

In this chapter we will discuss:

- assessing staff requirements
- deciding between permanent or temporary
- writing job specifications
- how to recruit
- preparing interview schedules
- conducting interviews
- making the right choices
- giving first day support and advice.

ASSESSING STAFF REQUIREMENTS

The saying that 'small is beautiful' is very relevant to staffing levels. More staff than needed can mean that profits disappear in salaries, and workers become bored and disenchanted because they do not have enough to do. Conversely, of course, too few staff can have an equally bad effect on everyone. Stress levels rise, job satisfaction diminishes and working standards deteriorate.

What is needed is a careful evaluation of what level of worker is needed where. If the office is a newly created one, start with as few staff as possible until you can judge how the business is developing. In an existing office, a new recruit should be taken on only when it is apparent that your current staff are not coping with the workload. Even then, before recruiting, check that everyone is doing his or her job to the best of their ability, and that time is not being wasted due to insufficient training or staff being unaware of what is expected of them.

DECIDING BETWEEN PERMANENT OR TEMPORARY

Once the decision has been taken to recruit one or more members of staff, you then have to think about whether your needs are likely to be permanent or not.

A permanent member of staff, either full or part time, is entitled to be paid for sick leave and holidays, plus any special benefits, such as a pension or annual bonus that your organisation may offer to its employees.

Temporary staff, again either full or part time, can either be employed by you direct or can be supplied by an agency. Many businesses are choosing to employ their own temps, often on a fixed term contract of say six months, as this works out much cheaper than paying an agency. For instance, you could have to pay an agency £6.00 an hour, or even more, for a temp who is only earning £4.00 an hour.

Apart from their obvious use when covering for holidays and sickness, the employment of temps is so popular nowadays because they are not normally entitled to any of the usual benefits. They just get paid for the hours they work. Also, if the workload decreases a temp can be dismissed without any problem, whereas a permanent member of staff is a lot harder to get rid of. With the uncertainty surrounding the viability of a great number of businesses today, employing temps is the only sensible answer to any staff shortages that arise from time to time.

WRITING JOB DESCRIPTIONS

Before recruiting permanent staff a job description should be prepared so that it is clear to both you and prospective employees what is required of them. This job description is generally sent out in advance of an interview.

If an accurate job description is prepared and agreed with a prospective employee, then both you and they will know what is expected of them. The frequent cry of 'I'm not doing that because it is not my job', can be dealt with immediately by both parties taking a look at the job description. It should be mentioned, however, that many employers get round the problem of job descriptions being 'law' by adding a sentence at the bottom saying something like 'These duties may be amended from time to time at the discretion of the management'.

A typical job description is shown in figure 4.

WRITING JOB SPECIFICATIONS

Whereas the **job description** identifies the nature of the job on offer, the

THE SWAN GROUP OF HOTELS
Job description

Job title: Receptionist/WP Operator
Responsible to: Hotel Manager
Place of work: The Ship Hotel
Salary scale: £8,000-10,000 pa
Days of work: Monday to Friday
Hours of work: Wk 1 – 0700 hrs-1400 hrs
                            Wk 2 – 1400 hrs-2100 hrs
Holiday entitlement: 4 weeks pa, plus public holidays

Duties and responsibilities

1. Answering the telephone, operating the switchboard, and making calls where necessary.

2. Dealing with bookings for both hotel accommodation and restaurant.

3. Receiving and assisting visitors to the hotel.

4. Undertaking the typing of letters, memos, reports and menus, plus any other documents requested by the Hotel Manager.

5. Providing relief cover when other members of staff are away, if acceptable to the employee. These extra hours are not compulsory.

These duties may be amended from time to time at the discretion of the Hotel Manager.

May 19XX

Fig. 4. A typical job description.

job specification identifies the type of employee required to fill that job. The job specification should be produced after the job description.

The easiest way of producing a job specification is to prepare a master copy listing the headings applicable to all vacancies. Then, when a vacancy occurs, a copy of that master can be produced and filled in as appropriate.

The job specification should give a perfect profile of the person best suited for the job. This can then be used first of all at the CV stage and later at the interview to match each candidate with that perfect profile. Unfortunately, however, nothing in life is ever perfect and usually the person who comes closest to the job specification criteria will be selected.

Figures 5 and 6 show a standard blank job specification form and then a copy of this form filled in for the vacancy at The Ship Hotel.

HOW TO RECRUIT

The main ways of recruiting permanent staff are by:

- word of mouth or personal recommendation
- using an agency
- contacting the local Jobcentre
- placing an advertisement in the newspaper
- advertising in local radio
- liaising with schools, colleges and universities.

Word of mouth or personal recommendation
This method, although sometimes useful, is rather limiting, as the general public will never find out that the job vacancy exists. On the other hand, if one valued employee recommends someone to you, that other person could turn out to be a genuinely good find. You should use your judgement to decide whether or not you have cast your net wide enough.

Using an agency
If you use an agency to recruit your staff you will have to pay heftily for the privilege. Most agencies charge the employer a percentage of the employee's first year's salary.

What many agencies will do, however, is sift through the hundreds of applications that normally arrive for any vacancy and provide you with a shortlist of suitable candidates. This can save you a considerable amount of time, and in business 'time is money'.

JOB SPECIFICATION

Job title:

Responsible to:

Place of work:

Age range:

Educational background
and qualifications:

Skills and personal
qualities required:

Previous work
experience:

Health record:

Fig. 5. A blank job specification.

JOB SPECIFICATION

Job title: Receptionist/WP Operator

Responsible to: Hotel Manager

Place of work: The Ship Hotel

Age range: 18-25 years

Educational background and qualifications:	Educated to GCSE standard (or equivalent) with good passes in English, Maths and either French or German. RSA Typewriting Skills Stage II RSA Word Processing Stage II
Skills and personal qualities required:	Well groomed appearance. Able to work on own initiative. Good telephone manner. Ability to get on with members of the public and work colleagues. Needs to speak French or German.
Previous work experience:	None necessary as full training will be given.
Health record:	Check applicant is in good general health. Arrange medical examination. No spotty faces!

Fig. 6. A completed job specification.

The Jobcentre

Using the Jobcentre can save time too, although they will obviously not spend as much time selecting suitable candidates as a private agency. They will advertise your position though and talk to anyone interested in applying, assessing whether, in theory, they would be suitable.

Placing an advertisement in the newspaper

This is perhaps the most common way of recruiting staff. An advertisement is displayed, either in a local or national newspaper, inviting interested applicants to respond in writing or by telephone. It is important to describe the job vacancy accurately, so that theoretically only those who are able to carry out the duties expected of them will apply. In practice there will unfortunately always be the odd one or two who will insist on applying for a job totally unsuited to their skills.

This is a suggested newspaper advertisement for the job described in figure 6:

> Receptionist/WP Operator required for busy hotel. Age range 18-25 years. Shift hours, Monday to Friday. Applicant must be interested in meeting people, articulate, well presented and willing to assist with word processing duties when required. GCSE passes in English, Maths and either German or French, plus RSA Typewriting Skills and Word Processing Stage II. Please send a handwritten letter and typed CV to Sally Wornes, Manager, The Ship Hotel, Barstock, Middlesex BA23 9YH. Closing date 21 May 19XX.

The advertisement is clear, explains exactly what is required and how to go about applying. Always give a closing date so that interviews are not delayed for too long.

Advertising on local radio

This can be an expensive method, especially if you need to give the listeners constant reminders of what you have to offer, should they decide to register their interest. Some local stations do, however, have special 'Jobfinder' sections in their programmes.

Liaising with schools, colleges and universities

These establishments can be very worthwhile places to try for your staff, depending on the level of the positions you have on offer. Always liaise with the teachers or lecturers first, even if you know the person you would like to take on for your office.

PREPARING INTERVIEW SCHEDULES

Assuming you are the one going through the CVs and arranging the interviews, the first task to carry out is to sort the CVs into three piles. The first pile can be the definite 'Yes's', the second pile the 'Not sure's' and the third pile the definite 'No's'. Use the job specification to assist you.

Look through the 'Not sure' pile again. Put the most promising ones into the 'Yes' pile and the others with the 'No's'. Next, write to the 'No's' expressing your regret at having to turn down their applications. (See figure 7.)

This process should narrow down the applicants to a reasonable number. Write to each one of them offering an interview day and time. (See figure 8.) Give plenty of notice if at all possible. Make sure you are not cramming too many interviews into one day, and be prepared to find alternative dates for anyone who cannot attend at their allotted time. Prepare an interview list as soon as you receive the replies.

As far as references are concerned, some businesses ask for them in advance of the interview, and other wait until afterwards. They are usually only a formality anyway, but they can hold up the selection process if referees are slow to reply.

CONDUCTING INTERVIEWS

A good interview is well planned and structured in advance. Using the individual CVs and your job specification form you should be able to compile a number of questions to ask each applicant in advance. It is important also to remember that you are not there for a 'chat', you are there to appoint someone to a job. Set a time limit for each interview and keep to it.

Opinions are divided on the layout of the interview room. Generally speaking, unless the interview is very formal, it is far better to have you and your interviewee sitting in comfortable chairs around a small table rather than you sitting one side of your desk and them facing you. This can create an unnecessary barrier. Informality is more likely to offer you the chance to get to know the 'real' person.

The Ship Hotel
Barstock
Middlesex
BA23 9XH

26 May 19XX

Miss J Smith
Rose Cottage
Barstock
Middx
BA14 7YH

Dear Miss Smith

Receptionist/WP Operator

Thank you for sending us your CV and letter of application for the above vacancy.

We have received several hundred applications, and have found considerable difficulty in selecting just a few people for interview. We are sorry to say that on this occasion your application was not successful.

Thank you for your interest in our hotel and may we wish you every success in the future.

Yours sincerely

Sally Wornes
HOTEL MANAGER

Fig. 7. Letter to applicants not being interviewed.

The Ship Hotel
Barstock
Middlesex
BA23 9XH

26 May 19XX

Miss P Jones
35 The Street
Barstock
Middx
BA12 9YN

Dear Miss Jones

Receptionist/WP Operator

Thank you for sending your CV and application form for the above vacancy.

We are pleased to invite you for interview on Wednesday 10 June at 0930 hrs. Perhaps you would confirm to us that you are able to attend.

After the interview we shall require you to take a short test using the WordPerfect 5.1 word processing package. Do not worry if you are not familiar with this particular package. We just want to see that you are able to produce an error free document in a competent manner.

We look forward to meeting you.

Your sincerely

Sally Wornes
HOTEL MANAGER

Fig. 8. Letter to applicants invited for interview.

If you are not experienced at interviewing you will probably feel a little nervous at first. Remember, however, that your interviewee will be feeling far more nervous than you, and it is your responsibility to put them at their ease.

Interviewing — a step-by-step guide
When conducting an interview, follow this step-by-step guide:

- Welcome the interviewee with a smile and handshake. Introduce yourself, and invite the person to sit down. Offer refreshments, especially if the interviewee has travelled some distance.

- Begin with general conversation: the weather, the journey, a hobby or interest mentioned on the CV, anything that will put the person at ease.

- Explain what the job entails, even though the interviewee has received a job description.

- Work through your list of questions in a logical way. Use 'open ended' questions as much as possible. These are questions which require more than a 'yes' or 'no' in answer. For example: 'Tell me why you would like this job?'.

- Use 'closed' or direct questions when direct answers are required. For example: 'Would you be prepared to work extra hours if necessary?'

- **Always** make notes as the interview progresses. Never rely on your memory. After interviewing ten people, your memory will definitely be rather muddled!

- Show an interest in what your interviewee says. Nod, smile and use encouraging words.

- Remember to ask the interviewee if he or she has any questions to ask you. Give the fullest answers you can to those questions.

- When all relevant points have been covered on both sides, thank the interviewee for attending and say when you expect to be in touch with them.

● If a test of any sort is being taken, arrange this at the end of the interview.

MAKING THE RIGHT CHOICES

After the interviews you should know who you wish to appoint to the position. You might, however, still be undecided. If you have not yet taken up references, then now is the time to do so. These references might help you to make up your mind. Should you still be undecided then the next step is to arrange for second interviews to take place.

Second interviews are normally more informal because you have already spoken with the interviewees. Prepare some different questions, perhaps a few awkward ones, which might help you to come to a decision. If you still cannot reach a decision after these interviews, it would be as well to re-advertise the position and start again.

Assuming that a decision is reached, either after the first or second interviews, the next step is to notify the successful applicant in writing — even if you do 'phone them first to give them the good news. Often enclosed with such a letter is the **contract of employment**, which clearly sets out what is expected of the new employee, and what they can expect in return. An example of a letter of appointment is shown in figure 9.

Once the job offer has been accepted you should then write to the unsuccessful applicants explaining to them that the vacancy has been filled, see figure 10.

GIVING FIRST DAY SUPPORT AND ADVICE

Anyone starting a new job feels nervous and apprehensive. No doubt you have been through it yourself, so you will know what it is like. When you are taking on a new member of staff it is important that you offer time, patience and understanding to that person on the first day, and also throughout the following few weeks. This will help both of you. You will more readily gain a happy, useful employee, and they will feel wanted and able to cope with the job.

Try to find time for all the following on that first day:

● a welcoming greeting.

● a friendly chat about life in general, with the aim of finding out a little more about the new person in your office.

The Ship Hotel
Barstock
Middlesex
BA23 9XH

11 June 19XX

Miss P Jones
35 The Street
Barstock
Middx
BA12 9YN

Dear Miss Jones

Receptionist/WP Operator

Further to our telephone conversation yesterday, I am delighted to confirm your appointment as Receptionist/WP Operator at our Hotel, commencing on 1 July 19XX at 0700 hrs.

You will find enclosed two copies of our Contract of Employment. Please sign and return one copy to us as soon as possible. Once I have received your signed Contract, an appointment will be made for you to have a medical, and I will telephone you to arrange a day for this.

Your hours of work are: Week 1, 0700 hrs-1400 hrs and Week 2, 1400 hrs-2100 hrs. Holiday entitlement is 4 weeks each year, plus public holidays. You will serve a probationary period of three months, during which time your salary will be £8,000 per annum. After satisfactory completion of the probationary period your salary will rise to £9,000 per annum. One month's notice is required if you wish to leave the hotel.

I look forward to welcoming you to The Ship and hope that you will be very happy with us.

Yours sincerely

Sally Wornes
HOTEL MANAGER

enc

Fig. 9. Letter of appointment.

**The Ship Hotel
Barstock
Middlesex
BA23 9XH**

15 June 19XX

Miss S Platt
28 Woolpack Road
Barstock
Middx
BA9 0LF

Dear Miss Platt

Receptionist/WP Operator

Thank you very much for attending for interview last week. We are sorry to say, however, that on this occasion you were not successful.

We had an unprecedented response to our advertisement reflecting, no doubt, the effects of the present recession. This meant we found it very hard to choose just one person from the many applicants, yourself included, who had the experience, qualifications and personality we were looking for.

We do wish you every success in finding a suitable position. If we advertise a vacancy here in the future, please feel free to apply, and we will consider your application very seriously.

Yours sincerely

Sally Wornes
HOTEL MANAGER

Fig. 10. Letter rejecting an applicant following interview.

- a tour of the office or offices, introducing everyone and explaining what they do.

- a resume of the job the new person is there to do. Start your training process, taking one stage at a time, and trying not to offload too much information at once.

- answers to a never ending barrage of questions, even though you may think many of them are elementary and unnecessary.

- a sympathetic attitude to your newcomer.

Always remember that if that first day goes well, the succeeding days are likely to go well too, so make sure you both go home happy at the end of it!

CHECKLIST

- Are you sure that you need to take on extra staff?

- Do you need full-timers, part-timers, permanent or temporary staff?

- Have you prepared a satisfactory job description and job specification?

- How are you going to recruit?

- Have you matched the job specification to your applicants' CVs?

- Have you acknowledged unsuccessful applications?

- Have you written to the people you want to interview?

- Are you happy about the interview room?

- Are you going to conduct a well structured interview, with questions prepared in advance?

- Are you confident of making the right choices?

- Have you written to the successful and unsuccessful applicants?

- Are you prepared to devote plenty of time to your new staff?

CASE STUDIES

Dorothy resists change

One of Dorothy's part-timers has handed in her notice as she does not like the new, go-ahead headmistress, Miss Porter. It is being left to Dorothy to find a replacement, with the proviso that someone under 45 must be chosen!

Dorothy does not know where to start. The two staff have been there as long as her. In the end she goes into the Jobcentre and they are very helpful, telling her that they will find some suitable applicants and refer them on to the school.

Dorothy is very good at administration and has no trouble sending out interview letters once Miss Porter has sifted through the CVs. She is, however, horrified to be asked to conduct the interviews. Miss Porter feels it is important for Dorothy to have someone she can get on with.

Unfortunately Dorothy does not like any of the applicants. They are all far too young and threatening! She tells Miss Porter that she has found them all unsuitable and they then advertise in the local paper. To everyone's relief a lady of 40 eventually presents herself in a favourable light, but Dorothy has proved by this exercise that she is likely to have a negative attitude to Miss Porter's ideas of updating the office in the future.

Sue chooses her temps

Sue now has a number of company personnel officers ready to meet her, so she decides it is time to find her 'temps'. She has quite a few contacts including a very good training school nearby. She approaches them and they suggest a number of people to her. As a backup she also advertises in the local paper. She asks everyone to send her a CV and a handwritten letter explaining why they would like to work for her.

The response is overwhelming, over 200 applications, and Sue finds it a hard job sifting through all the CVs. To help her she writes herself a job specification as follows:

Job specification — Office temps
This specification shows the minimum requirements for all staff.
Some positions may require a higher standard.

Age range:	25-50 years
Educational background and qualifications:	Good general level of education required with English Langauge at GCE or GCSE level. RSA or Pitman Examinations in typing, and word processing up to Advanced Level. Shorthand or audio experience an advantage.
Skills and personal qualities required:	Word processing experience a must. Ability to mix well with people. No family ties that will preclude working.
Previous work experience:	Previous office experience a must (at least 2 yrs).

By stating the age range and minimum qualifications and experience required, Sue manages to cut the CVs by more than half. The rest she goes through again and selects 30 people for interview. She conducts the interviews over a period of a week, as she also gives each applicant a very strict typing and word processing test which takes time. Fifteen people are finally accepted.

Three months after her initial permissions were granted Sue is ready to begin her new business venture. Fortunately for her it is now the middle of spring, just about the best time for temps to find employment, so she is hopeful of a successful start.

POINTS FOR DISCUSSION

1.   What are the advantages and disadvantages to the **employee** of being a permanent member of staff?

2.   Do you see the number of part-time jobs increasing or decreasing in years to come? Give reasons for your answer.

3.   Do you think it is fair to appoint a member of staff through personal recommendation? Again, give reasons for your answer.

4
Taking Over an Office

It is never easy taking over an office from someone else. If that person was very popular, you are likely to be resented at first. If they were bad at their job, you will be left to clear up the mess. It may be that you have worked under your predecessor and already know your working colleagues. On the other hand, they may be complete strangers to you.

In this chapter we will discuss:

● treading carefully
● overcoming resentment
● taking over a disaster
● learning the office systems
● introducing 'house rules'
● making changes
● monitoring progress
● achieving targets
● being accepted.

TREADING CAREFULLY

When you take over an office from someone else you must remember that it will take time before you are accepted and respected. It is, however, possible to make your first few weeks at least bearable, if not enjoyable, if you follow these suggestions.

● Do not go straight into the job and want to change everything. Give yourself and your staff time to adjust.

● Avoid at all costs a 'them and us' situation developing between your working colleagues and yourself.

- Speak to your staff, individually and as a group, and explain to them that you do not intend to upset the 'status quo'.

- Learn what goes on by watching and listening.

- Keep a look out for any internal disputes.

OVERCOMING RESENTMENT

By the end of the first week you might well have the impression that your predecessor, Mr X or Mrs Y, was a saint! Indeed, should you be taking over from someone who was very popular, you will have a particularly hard time at first.

It is up to you to understand the resentment and try not to let it upset you. After all, it is nothing personal. The chances are that your colleagues cannot yet judge whether you are going to be better, worse, nicer or nastier than the person you are replacing. It is just a case of 'better the devil you know'!

As long as you do your job as well as you are able, and spend time getting to know your staff (if you do not already know them), the resentment will gradually disappear. Who knows, when you eventually move on to pastures new, they might well say the same complimentary things about you as they are now saying about Mr X or Mrs Y!

TAKING OVER A DISASTER

On the other hand it is equally possible that you will be taking over an office that has been running disastrously for some time under your predecessor. This might be because he or she allowed the staff to be lax and lazy in their working methods, letting them go home early in the afternoons, take all day to do a simple task, and generally do as they please. Or perhaps no one, including the previous manager, knew what they were doing, resulting in an unfulfilled, unhappy staff with no sense of purpose or direction.

Either way, it is up to you from Day One to let everyone see that you are going to be **different**. That you want to see an efficiently run office, where the staff are happy, fulfilled and fully occupied, and all working towards the same common goal. This might seem rather idealistic at first, but it is what you should strive to achieve for everyone's sake.

LEARNING THE OFFICE SYSTEMS

If this particular office environment is new to you then finding out about the systems used can be a very good way of getting to know the staff. It will make them feel useful and wanted if you ask them to show you various aspects of their job.

If possible, try out all the different systems for yourself. Learn how to use the word processing package, do accounts on the computer and operate the filing system.

Take time out just to sit and watch too. By observing what everyone is up to you will soon be able to judge how efficiently the office is running and where, later on, you will need to make changes.

INTRODUCING HOUSE RULES

Once you have had a good look around you for a few weeks, you should feel ready to set your own 'house rules'. Always approach the introduction of new 'rules' with more than a little tact and diplomacy: for example, 'I know Mr Black used to say lunch breaks could be taken at the same time, but I would like to try staggering them so that the telephone is covered. Perhaps we could try it for a couple of weeks to see how it works out.'

Where hero worship for your predecessor is hard to shift, quietly point out, whenever necessary, that you are sure Mr X or Mrs Y did a wonderful job, but that they are no longer running the office, you are, and that you have your own working methods.

In situations where your staff have been allowed to do as they please in the past, try to show by example that you will not tolerate inefficient and shoddy working methods. Emphasise the hours of work and how important it is for everyone to stick to them. Say to them that the job situation is such that no one can be complacent. Efficiency must be maintained if the company or organisation is to survive in today's competitive market. Play on their better nature. Make them feel they will benefit and so will all their colleagues if a good day's work is put in **every** day.

MAKING CHANGES

Fundamental changes to working methods are slightly different from 'house rules'. Here we are talking about changing how the various systems are run. Perhaps even changing who does what job.

Never make changes just to make your mark. If a system of, say, dealing with the post, has been working perfectly well up until now, then there is no point in changing it.

Where you do intend to make changes, spend time explaining to the staff involved why these changes are taking place and that you think they will be for the better. Involve the staff in what is going on and instill confidence in them that their future will be more secure if office efficiency improves. Train them properly, so that they do not have difficulty in understanding your new working methods. If they don't understand, they will feel threatened and this will lead to non-co-operation and a bad office atmosphere.

MONITORING PROGRESS

It is very easy to get so caught up in the excitement of managing your office that you lose sight of your aims. You are not just there to show everyone that you are their 'boss'. You are there to make the running of the office as smooth and efficient as possible.

After a month or so, sit back and assess the situation. Ask yourself these questions:

● Has your first month been successful?
● Have you made any changes?
● Have they been successful?
● Are your staff happy?
● Are they all fully occupied?
● Do you involve them enough in your decision making?
● Have you achieved as much as you had hoped?
● Are you convinced that the office is operating as, if not more, efficiently than it was under your predecessor?

If you can truthfully answer 'yes' to all these questions then you can consider your first month to have been a success! Just make sure that you are not kidding yourself!

ACHIEVING TARGETS

Most businesses today operate with targets to achieve. Your own targets may be set by your boss or they may be set by you, depending on whether you are the boss or you are answerable to someone else.

Let us look at an example:

Sally West works as the Telesales Office Manager for Mark Adams in his double glazing company (see Chapter 2). Mark sets Sally targets for each month. These targets are based on the number of firm appointments her team is able to make for Mark to call on. The first three months results could look like this:

January
Target figure: 30 appointments
Target achieved: 22 appointments (4 orders)

February
Target figure: 30 appointments
Target achieved: 32 appointments (9 orders)

March
Target figure: 40 appointments
Target achieved: 40 appointments (4 orders)

Mark has tried increasing the target figures in March as February was very successful. The low number of actual orders in March suggests, however, that perhaps the staff have felt under pressure and tried to book anyone up for an appointment, even if they were not seriously interested in double glazing.

In general targets are a good thing. Everyone knows what they have to achieve and in many organisations they also know that if they continually under-achieve they will lose their jobs.

Whether you set targets for your staff and yourself, or targets are set for you, they should be treated seriously. With some jobs, such as sales reps, targets reached or exceeded can mean more money earned in commission, which is obviously an incentive, but the overall advantage of achieving targets is keeping your job and that is normally the biggest incentive of all.

BEING ACCEPTED

Almost everyone likes to be liked. There are not many of us who can honestly say we do not care what other people think or feel about us. Because we spend so many of our waking hours at work, being liked and respected there is almost as important as what goes on in our home life.

Taking over an office from someone else will normally put you at a temporary disadvantage as far as being liked is concerned, especially if your staff did not want a change in the first place, or did not consider you to be the best person for the job. You have got to earn their respect gradually. You can do this by showing that you do not class yourself as someone special or better than them. You are just there to do a job, and to help them do their jobs too.

Make your staff feel that you care about them. Ask about 'little Johns's asthma problems' if you have been told about them. Remember birthdays and join in with the celebrations. Even though you are managing the office, you can still let your hair down occasionally. In fact it will make you seem more human and ordinary, and that is when you will start to be accepted for what and who you are.

Don't be too impatient though. Being accepted in any situation takes time, and in no instance is this more true than when you are stepping into someone else's shoes.

CHECKLIST

When taking over an office from someone else, remember to:

● take your time to settle in

● learn what goes on by watching and listening

● ask the staff to show you their jobs

● let them see that you are an individual and therefore have different ideas to your predecessor

● not make changes just for the sake of it

● assess your progress from time to time

● make sure you are keeping to any set targets you may have

● do your best to get on well with the staff and become accepted by them.

CASE STUDIES

Stephen keeps his temper

Although Stephen is thrilled to be working in his estate agent's office in rural Suffolk rather than in busy, smog filled, London, he is very apprehensive about taking over from Mr Baines, his predecessor. Bob Baines was loved by everyone, staff and local residents alike. He was a Suffolk man too, unlike Stephen.

The first day goes badly. Stephen has two negotiators and two typists to manage. The two negotiators, one male and one female, delight in telling him how Bob used to leave them to their own devices entirely. Stephen knows the office's results have been disastrous over the last couple of years and secretly thinks that is the reason why, but he doesn't say anything for now. The two typists are 50 plus, very good 'buddies' and treat Stephen as though he has just left kindergarten. He finds himself running short on temper at times.

The office systems are archaic. One of the typists still uses a manual typewriter and refuses to change! The photocopier is ancient, and there is no fresh ground coffee in sight. Stephen despairs!

Two weeks into the job and Stephen is left wondering whether he has made the right decision after all. However, he looks forward to expanding and reorganising the office and hopes that he will be able to reorganise the staff too.

John wins over his staff

John's life at the hospital is not running too smoothly either. He was quite happy in the admin department, a little cog in a big wheel, without any real worries in life. His new position in charge of the administration of outpatients is going to be, he soon discovers, quite different.

John has the added problem of the imminent move to larger premises. This is not for six months, but does prevent him from really settling into a routine.

There are 30 full and part-time staff working in outpatients. It takes John the first couple of weeks just to get to know them all by name. Their previous 'boss' was a woman, and as most of the department is staffed by women, he finds a certain amount of hesitation in accepting a man for the job.

A plus point for John is that he has been at the hospital for years, and although he was working in an entirely different section he does at least know his way around. He also has a very pleasant, easy going personality, with a good sense of humour and this helps him to cope at the beginning.

John makes a point of asking all the staff to show him what they do. He explains that this is not because he doubts their ability, rather that he wants to learn exactly what goes on in Outpatients. Most of the staff are co-operative, although they still treat him with reservation.

At the end of the first fortnight John calls a meeting of all his staff, partly to tell them of the office move in six months' time, but also to thank them for their support to date. Everyone finds this rather pleasing. They appreciate the trouble John has taken to show that they are important and that he appreciates their efforts.

POINTS FOR DISCUSSION

1. Do you think that if you take over an office you should show your staff who is 'boss' from the very beginning?

2. Your predecessor was dismissed for drinking heavily, failing to reach targets, and swindling the company funds, yet all the staff in the accounts office loved him and say he was unfairly dismissed. What would you say to the staff at the meeting you call on the first day? If possible, work with a partner on this one, both of you giving your views on how to handle such a situation.

3. You are in charge of managing a busy sales office. Through sheer hard work you have been promoted to this position at a very young age — 23. All the staff are older than you and resent your position. How would you prove to them that you are capable of doing the job?

5
Managing an Office

Managing an office successfully is not an easy task, but it can be a very rewarding one, providing that you understand exactly what kind of a person you need to be in order to succeed.

In this chapter we will discuss:

- believing in yourself
- adopting the right attitude
- exercising leadership
- becoming creative
- using effective body language
- learning to delegate
- problem solving
- taking time out
- avoiding stress

BELIEVING IN YOURSELF

In Chapter 1 we looked at the qualities necessary to succeed in managing an office. Figure 1 narrowed these qualities down to single words or short phrases, and no doubt by now you will have decided how many of these apply to you — hopefully most of them!

Above everything else, anyone involved in managing anything must believe in their ability to succeed. For if you do not think positively, how can you expect anyone working with you to think positively? It is up to you to instil confidence in those around you. At times you might not feel confident, but you must portray a confident image, and you **must** at all times believe that you and they **can** succeed in the end.

Nothing in life is straightforward and simple, but just think of the satisfaction and sense of achievement you will feel if you succeed in managing your office efficiently and profitably.

ADOPTING THE RIGHT ATTITUDE

The dictionary definition of attitude is 'a way of thinking and behaving'. To adopt the right attitude when managing an office the word 'positive' needs to be inserted, *ie* 'a positive way of thinking and behaving'.

In most office situations you will be involved with the following people:

- your own working colleagues
- colleagues from other organisations
- visitors
- clients.

Although your approach or attitude might be slightly different when dealing with each of these categories, remember the three p's. You should *always* be:

- polite
- positive
- persuasive.

An attitude problem

Some people are said to have an 'attitude problem'. This basically means that they think and behave in a way that is unacceptable to others. Often, although not by any means always, such people come from an unstable background, or have had to compete with brainy or very popular brothers and sisters.

An 'attitude problem' is very difficult, firstly to identify and admit to, and then to overcome. Think carefully about the way you approach the people you deal with at work, and make sure that you are treating them in the right way. Some managers and bosses gain a reputation for being 'bullies'. They let a little bit of power go to their heads. A bully is never liked or respected. A bully is unlikely to manage an office successfully. Check your attitude and, if necessary, change it for a more positive one.

EXERCISING LEADERSHIP

It is very important for you to show good leadership skills when managing your office. Your aim should be to create a 'team' with you as a part of that team, rather than 'you' as the manager and 'them' as the workers.

Teamwork is what effective management is all about. You need to show your team that you are:

- enthusiastic
- encouraging
- willing to accept responsibility
- well motivated
- not afraid to learn yourself
- firm, but at the same time understanding
- able to cope in a crisis.

It is up to you to see that every member of your team knows what is expected of them. Try to 'show' what is needed by good example rather than 'tell' in a dictatorial manner.

The impression you give to your team can mean the difference between co-operation and rebellion. If you do not seem to know what you are doing, you will not motivate your team. Instead, they will do as little as possible and the office will quickly become disorganised with everyone blaming someone else when mistakes are made.

Good leadership skills take time, patience and skill to develop but are essential for the effective management of people.

BECOMING CREATIVE

The dictionary defines the word create as 'to bring into existence out of nothing', or 'to originate'. Managing an office definitely requires a creative mind. This will enable you to:

- constantly come up with new ideas
- try those ideas out
- think about different angles
- motivate others with your enthusiasm
- keep the office environment 'alive'
- plan for the future.

If you are to be creative, you will need to get into the habit of always carrying around a notepad or pocket dictaphone to record your ideas as you have them. Never rely on memory. When you lead a busy life your memory is often not as good as you would like, because you are having to concentrate on so many things at once.

Encourage others to have creative thoughts too. 'Two heads are better than one' is often the case. Bounce ideas off one another, either at a meeting or just across the office desk. Ideas should never be discouraged even if they are not eventually adopted. Without ideas and a creative mind, businesses die. Make sure that your office thrives because of new ideas and new innovations being constantly introduced.

USING EFFECTIVE BODY LANGUAGE

Body language, or non-verbal communication, means the way we communicate with others by using different parts of our body as well as, or instead of, speaking to them. It shows the emotional side of our relationships.

The messages we convey by means of body language are often far more meaningful than any words that may be spoken. These messages can be deliberate, such as a frown, a shrug of the shoulders or looking away when spoken to, or they can be involuntary, such as a shiver.

It is very important that the body language you show is interpreted in the way you want it to be. For instance, although you might feel very irritated indeed when a member of your staff fails to carry out an instruction in the right way, if you look up at the ceiling in annoyance and glower at the person concerned, you will not do a lot to promote good staff relations! Far better to speak to the person, face to face, establishing eye contact, and explain to them patiently what you are upset about, thus giving that person an opportunity to answer without feeling threatened or inadequate.

Similarly, most of you will, at some time, have had to sit through a boring conversation with someone you dislike, just to be polite. In business this happens often, and in such a situation you cannot afford to let your body language show. After all, that boring conversation might lead to an important business deal. If you can at least pretend to be interested in what is being said by looking the person in the eye, nodding and giving the occasional smile, rather than by yawning and falling asleep, you are less likely to upset your client and more likely to clinch the deal.

LEARNING TO DELEGATE

Managing an office is a complex and diverse business and, unless you run your office all on your own, learning to delegate successfully might well be the most useful tool of management you ever use. Unfortunately, of course, if you work on your own there is nobody to delegate to.

Assuming you do employ staff, however, it is up to you to work out an effective delegation programme so that everyone in your team is using their skills in the best possible way. Time is money and if, for instance, you spend half the day on the 'phone finding out where the photocopier repair man has got to, rather than speaking to an important business client, then your time has not been utilised in the most profitable way.

Delegation can be a problem area for managers, as many think that they can do all the work better themselves, and that there is no need for them to delegate at all. In fact, however, effective delegation can be beneficial for all concerned. If properly carried out it can:

● counteract boredom amongst the staff
● give everyone a sense of purpose
● create a friendly working environment
● improve overall efficiency
● prevent any one person (usually you) from becoming overworked.

How to delegate
1. Decide on task or tasks to be delegated.
2. Work out who is going to take over those tasks.
3. Check out that person's existing workload.
4. Speak to the person concerned and ask for their views.
5. If they are happy to take on the extra task(s), train them accordingly.
6. Monitor their progress.
7. Delegate further, if appropriate.

Try not to be stubborn over delegation. Remember that by delegating certain tasks you will have more time to spend on managing your office efficiently. Also, your working colleagues will feel that, quite rightly, you see them as useful members of your team and that you trust their abilities sufficiently to give them more responsibility.

PROBLEM SOLVING

Our problems in life, whether at home or at work, can sometimes seem insurmountable. Have you ever woken up in the morning, thought about your problems, and promptly felt really depressed even before setting foot out of bed? I'm sure most of us have at some time or another, but problems, once identified, can often be solved.

Five problem-solving steps

There are five steps to take when developing your problem-solving techniques:

1. Identify the problem. Get it clear in your mind what it is that is causing you worry.

2. Look at possible solutions.

3. Decide on the action you are going to take.

4. Take the appropriate action.

5. Assess whether you have now solved your problem. If not, try another possible solution!

Problems, if not solved, can be a major cause of stress. Facing up to problems as they arise, however, will counteract stress and promote a happy working environment for you and your staff.

TAKING TIME OUT

Managing an office takes a lot of time, energy and enthusiasm. It is vitally important, however, that you do not let your work take over your entire life. Being a dedicated hard working person is one thing, being obsessed by work is quite another.

Make sure that you keep your working and personal life quite separate, with sufficient time devoted to each. Resist the temptation to take work home, or to work late when it is not really necessary.

Are you in danger of becoming obsessed about work? Ask yourself these questions:

● Do you find yourself working late every evening?

● Do you take work home?

● Do you talk about work even when you are at home?

● Do you subconsciously plan for the next day at work when you are sitting watching TV or talking to your partner?

● Do you go to sleep at night and wake up in the morning thinking about work?

If you have answered 'yes' to these questions, then watch out! Your friends might start avoiding you, rather than listen to you droning on about your 'fascinating' job.

Those of you with families will find that your spare time can be taken up very easily, particularly if you have young children. Children grow up all too soon and if you spend every waking hour at work rather than dividing your time between your family and your job, you will miss all those years when they really need you.

Partners should be considered too. Many marriages break up when one or other partner becomes 'married' to a job and in consequence begins to ignore the person he or she once thought of as all important.

After thinking about everyone else, you should still leave a little time each week to think about yourself. You are important too, and at least a couple of hours a week should be spent in doing exactly what *you* want to do. For some that might be a night in the pub, for others a leisurely bath or a shopping spree. Anything that makes you feel good — just so long as it doesn't involve work and doesn't bankrupt you!

AVOIDING STRESS

More books have probably been written on 'stress' and related subjects in recent years than on almost any other topic! Stress is a very fashionable word. The dictionary definition of 'stress' gives us further fashionable words such as 'tension', 'strain' and 'pressure'.

Low levels of stress are often said to be beneficial rather than harmful. Working under pressure can make us perform better, with more to show for our efforts at the end of the week. What is not fully known, however, is just how much stress a person can take before he or she begins to suffer from psychological or physical side effects. Undeniably, executives and those in high pressure jobs do seem more prone to early heart attacks and blood pressure problems. Even certain types of cancers are said to be possibly stress related.

So, to be on the safe side, you should avoid getting 'stressed out' (more fashionable words!) at work. Concentrate on doing your job well, but do not put your health on the line. Life is short enough anyway without making it even shorter.

Controlling stress

Here are some tips to help you keep your stress levels under control at work:

- If you have a work related problem, discuss it with a colleague, partner or friend.

- Once you have a possible solution to your problem, act on it and then put it out of your mind.

- Do not try to do everything yourself. Delegate to other members of your staff.

- Work normal hours whenever you can. Avoid working long hours for several days in a row.

- Eat properly both at home and at work. Resist the temptation to skip meals.

- Take some exercise either before work, during the lunch break, or after work — every day if possible.

- Plan your days off and your holidays, so that you always have something to look forward to.

- If you do ever feel seriously under pressure, take a day off and get your life into perspective once more.

Remember above all that however good you are at your job, no one is indispensable. Enjoy your job, but give yourself a chance to enjoy the rest of your life too.

CHECKLIST

- Do you think you can succeed in managing your office?

- Are you prepared to work very hard to achieve your aims?

- Do you have a positive attitude towards other people?

- Are you working towards building an effective team?

- Do you make everyone feel equally important?

- Can you come up with creative ideas and put them into practice?

- Does your body language ever let you down?

- Are you prepared to delegate?

- Can you identify and deal with problems as they arise?

- Do you find time for your home as well as your working life?

- Are you aware of what stress is and how to avoid it?

CASE STUDIES

Dorothy is forced to delegate

As Dorothy is the only full-timer in the office and considers herself to be indispensable, she finds it very hard to delegate. Whereas April, her friend and working colleague of 25 years' standing, accepts Dorothy's little ways and is content to carry out all the mundane tasks, Wendy, the new part-timer, is not.

By the end of her second week, Wendy is threatening to leave unless she is given some responsible tasks to perform. Miss Porter, the headmistress, begins to lose patience with Dorothy and demands to be given a list of the duties that she and the part-timers carry out. Even Dorothy is surprised when she actually sets down on paper their various duties.

Dorothy
Typing Miss Porter's letters
Keeping her diary
Attending Governors' meetings and taking minutes
Typing Governors' correspondence
Arranging outings and overseas holidays
Typing PTA correspondence
Ordering and distributing stationery
Bookkeeping and accounts

April
Sending out of standard letters including duplicating
Checking registers
Typing the restaurant menus
Photocopying

Wendy
Typing internal rotas and notices

Answering the telephone
Filing
Making the tea and coffee.

Dorothy is issued with an ultimatum: either she shifts some of the tasks to her two members of staff or else she will be encouraged to take early retirement!

She succumbs, and gradually begins to realise that as a result she feels more able to cope with the modernisation of the office and its systems. Wendy, who has worked in a 'high tech' office before, offers to help with choosing the new equipment, and the three of them begin to work together as a team.

Sue neglects the family

Sue hasn't got any staff as such to help her in her office. Working from home and starting a new venture too has proved very difficult for her as she is constantly 'on the job'.

By the end of the summer, having had no holiday, Sue's husband and children are getting very fed up with the agency taking up her every waking moment. They feel left out, and she realises that she will have to be better organised.

Sue decides to prepare a timetable to use each week so that she has time set aside for everyone and everything. The business is up and running and it is no longer necessary for her to work such long hours. She begins to take the children to school again and arranges for one of her temps to cover her for a couple of hours each afternoon so that she can pick them up too. Up until now they have been met by a friend, who has looked after them for her, but she feels that it is time for her to take over the responsibility for her children again.

Sue gives a copy of the timetable to her husband who is immensely relieved that she intends to 'return' to them, and that he no longer has to take the children to school on his way to work. They also plan a weekend break to Euro Disney to help make up for their missed summer break.

Stephen throws his weight around

Stephen has a rebellion on his hands. In an all too familiar fit of temper he told both his typists, Margaret and Stephanie, that they needed to move towards the 21st century, not back to the Dark Ages! This was brought on by both of them refusing to use the shiny new computers and word processing packages that he had installed for them.

The company installing the machines gave the typists a very brief training session, which neither of them understood. He tells them that they are no use to him unless they can work the machines and does not stop to think that they are actually terrified of doing it wrong and making fools of themselves.

Vivien, one of the negotiators, steps in and tells Stephen in no uncertain terms that if he condescends to send Margaret and Stephanie on a proper training course maybe they will feel differently.

Stephen has an unfortunate way of upsetting people and he only goes along with them under sufferance. He would prefer to sack them all and start again rather than try to work with his existing staff. He has no respect at all for their feelings and how they would probably prefer to work without him too.

John listens to his staff

John is working hard on a new way to arrange the clinics so that there is not such a crowd of people waiting in the waiting rooms on certain days, while on others the clinic is empty. This means liaising with the various consultants and their secretaries, as well as with his own staff, who have been running the department for far longer than him.

As a first step John arranges a meeting of his own staff after work one day. When he asks them to come he puts it in such a way that they do not want to refuse. He makes them feel that they really will be contributing to the smooth running of the department if they attend. He has such a persuasive and appealing manner that everyone wants to co-operate with him. At the meeting he listens to them all and takes their ideas on board. He has discovered that if you treat your staff well and involve them in what is going on, they will do a far better job than if you treat them as inferior beings with no useful contribution to make.

POINTS FOR DISCUSSION

1. How important do you think it is to believe in your ability to succeed in whatever you do?

2. Do you know anyone with an attitude problem? How do they behave and how do you think they could improve?

3. Some people are said to be 'married' to their job. If they do not have a family or partner, do you think this matters?

6
Managing Office Staff

Employing staff can be both a pleasure and a headache. You will, no doubt, enjoy the occasional office outing, and the friendly chats that you have from time to time. On the other hand you are very unlikely to enjoy making someone redundant, or even worse, sacking a member of staff.

In this chapter we will discuss:

- keeping everyone happy
- training your staff
- dealing with problems
- organising staff appraisals
- arranging grievance interviews
- conducting a disciplinary interview
- dismissing someone
- making someone redundant
- planning staff outings.

KEEPING EVERYONE HAPPY

As we have said before, happy people perform well. Unhappy people do not. Although you will not be able to make everyone happy all of the time, especially since their worries may have nothing to do with their working environment, you should do your best to provide the best possible working conditions.

Keeping everyone happy really comes back to teamwork. Pulling together as a team, with every member of that team feeling useful, needed and involved, is necessary to create a happy, well run office. As team-leader it is up to you to see that everyone reaches their full potential and feels that their job is worthwhile.

TRAINING YOUR STAFF

Although it might well suit you for everyone to remain in the same job whilst you are in charge of the office, it might not suit your office staff. Many of them will be ambitious and will want or need to rise further up the office ladder of success.

Training opportunities will obviously vary according to the type of organisation you are working for. Large organisations such as councils, health authorities and many private companies offer expensive external courses on a regular basis to train their staff and give them the opportunity for advancement. If you are self-employed, and only employ a couple of staff, the outside training opportunities you can afford to offer will probably be minimal.

On-the-job training can, however, be offered to all staff, even if it is you who trains them. Before expecting a member of your staff to carry out a new task, always show them how you want it done. A few minutes of your time here and there could pay dividends later. If you install new equipment in the office, again either show the staff how to use it yourself or else arrange a training course for them. It is unreasonable of you to expect your staff to use equipment if they do not know how to operate it correctly. (See Stephen's case study in Chapter 4.)

Some organisations train all staff to do all jobs. A large provincial airport has tried this, and finds that it works very well. The terminal staff can step into each other's jobs whenever it is necessary. They say it creates more job satisfaction and largely eliminates the need to bring in extra staff when people are away. This is really an extension of the teamwork we discussed before.

DEALING WITH PROBLEMS

It would be unrealistic to say that if you create a perfect team and lead that team to the best of your ability, you will never have any staff problems. Human nature being what it is, problems are bound to arise when people work closely together.

When managing an office and its staff, always be on the lookout for changes in behaviour. Perhaps a usually sunny person will suddenly become withdrawn, or two normally happy workmates will fall out. If you do notice strange behaviour between one or more members of your staff:

- speak to the person or persons involved, privately

- try to establish exactly what the problem is

- if the problem is work-related, see if you can sort it out

- if the problem is personal, offer a sympathetic ear, but be very wary of offering advice

- monitor the situation carefully.

Make sure that no one member of your staff is desperately over-worked. Overwork can cause stress. Stress can cause health and behav-iourial problems. Such problems will then reflect on the rest of the staff and in time their work will be affected too.

ORGANISING STAFF APPRAISALS

Appraisals offer an opportunity to review the progress made by staff over a set period and to agree new targets for the future. This set period is often six months, but can be longer or shorter depending on circum-stances.

A staff appraisal usually takes the form of an interview.

Before the interview

- Contact the member of staff concerned and agree a date and time.

- Prepare notes to be used at the interview using the relevant personnel file.

At the interview

- Welcome the member of staff and make them feel at ease.

- Ask how they see their performance over the period in question.

- Listen carefully to the answers given and make relevant notes.

- Give your views on the staff member's performance.

- Praise any particularly commendable results.

- Query any poor results and ask why they occurred.

- Agree future targets and goals with the staff member.

Following the interview

●   Prepare a written letter or report and send a copy to the member of staff.

●   Make sure any agreed changes are implemented.

Take care to make appraisal interviews **constructive** rather than destructive. Even if performance has been poor, resist the temptation to 'lay into' your member of staff. Instead, try to find out the reason for the low standards, and ask forcefully but politely what they intend to do about it in the future. Conversely, if the member of staff has performed brilliantly, then say so. A little encouragement never did anyone any harm.

Where future targets are concerned, it is always better to agree these together, otherwise the person having to achieve them might feel they are unrealistic and this will cause bad feeling.

Well planned staff appraisals form a very important positive part of the relationship between a manager and staff.

ARRANGING GRIEVANCE INTERVIEWS

A grievance interview takes place when someone feels that he or she is being unfairly treated, by a colleague, or by the boss, or by the workplace in general. The single most important point for you to remember is that you must get to the truth, and sometimes this can be hard to do.

First of all you will need to interview the person who has a grievance. It is up to you to do all you can to put that person at their ease and to question them in such a way that you learn the information necessary to take some action. **Open ended** questions are best, *ie* 'what are these people actually saying to you?', rather than **closed** questions requiring one word answers, *ie* 'are these people talking about you?'

It is, of course, quite possible that it is you the person is complaining about. In that case it is down to you and you alone to sort the matter out. What is more likely, however, is that your staff member is being treated badly by a colleague, possibly because of resentment, jealousy, personal problems, or just to be plain awkward and nasty.

If another person is involved you will need to interview that person too. Get their side of the story and then, if necessary, bring the two sides together for a discussion with yourself as mediator.

In the vast majority of cases, simple discussion and a little understanding solves the problem entirely, particularly if you let both sides see that you are not prepared to tolerate unsociable and unkind behaviour.

CONDUCTING A DISCIPLINARY INTERVIEW

Disciplinary interviews are probably the least pleasant type of interview to conduct. They are necessary when a member of staff has acted in a way that is unacceptable to you or to the organisation you represent. As with a grievance interview, the most important aim is to get to the truth.

Even though you have arranged the interview because you are unhappy with a person's performance you should still start out by giving that person the benefit of the doubt. Greet them pleasantly and assure them that your interview will be strictly confidential.

One of the most common reasons for poor performance at work, late arrival, etc, is because of health or personal problems and this should be your first line of questioning. Someone who is worried about money, about his wife leaving him, or about his recently discovered heart condition will probably start behaving in an uncharacteristic way. That person will need understanding and sympathetic help, rather than threats about possible dismissal.

As the interview proceeds you should make notes, so that those notes can later be inserted into the personnel file. Establish a timescale for improvement and note this down too. Warn the member of staff that if there is no improvement in standards of behaviour, further action will be taken, with dismissal as the final outcome.

Try to finish the interview on a positive note, highlighting the person's good rather than bad points and saying that you are sure things will improve from now on. If things don't improve, however, a second interview will need to be arranged.

DISMISSING SOMEONE

If a person has been caught stealing the company funds, sexually assaulting a secretary, or carrying out other equally horrendous mischiefs, then he or she can be sacked without warning or notice. Such cases are, however, in the minority.

Normally, before sacking anyone, you will need to show by means of documentary evidence that you have tried all available means to correct a person's behaviour, and that all those attempts have failed. At least one **verbal** and two **written warnings** should be given to the member of staff, although in many cases two verbal warnings are offered before any written warning is sent. The verbal warnings will usually take the form of interviews, discussing the problems and trying to agree possible solutions. The written warnings will state the facts as they are, and copies must always be kept for the files, just in case the person claims unfair dismissal later on.

You should, of course, do all you can to help and assist, with a view to keeping, rather than losing, your staff member. If you do not succeed, however, then you are within your rights to give that person their notice or to pay them in lieu of notice and ask them to leave your employment.

It is unlikely that you will receive any claims for unfair dismissal, provided you carry out the disciplinary and dismissal procedures correctly, and give ample time between each of the warnings for the person concerned to mend their ways.

MAKING SOMEONE REDUNDANT

No one, unless they are very mercenary, likes to make an employee redundant. Unfortunately, however, there are occasions when this unpleasant task has to be undertaken.

Reasons for redundancy
Redundancy may be necessary for three main reasons:

1. because that person's job no longer exists, due to reorganisation etc
2. because of a decline in the volume of business
3. because the organisation or company is to close.

Assuming the reason to be 1 or 2, the best alternative is to find an employee who actually **wants** to be made redundant, who perhaps is willing to either take early retirement or to move to another organisation.

Should this not be possible, however, you will be forced to go ahead with enforcing redundancy on someone. The first thing to do is to make sure that you will be treating that person in a fair and just way. You must not, for instance, discriminate because of race or sex and you must pay that person adequate redundancy payments plus any holiday pay to which they are entitled.

Breaking the news
Present your facts and figures at a formal interview, explaining to your staff

member that you are only taking this course of action because you have to, and that it is in no way a reflection of their capability to do the job. Explain the financial implications and how any problems such as pension plans, life insurance and medical insurance will be dealt with. Impress on them that you will be more than happy to give them good references for any future job applications, and that should you be in a position to employ them again in the future you will contact them straight away.

Break the news as gently as you can. Many employees feel absolutely shattered when they are told they are to be made redundant, particularly if they have worked somewhere for many years. Because they might not absorb everything you have said first time, be prepared to discuss matters again with them in a day or so.

PLANNING STAFF OUTINGS

Whether or not you are involved in arranging outings or perhaps even holidays for your staff rather depends on how many staff you have!

Even the smallest office, however, with just two or three employees can be involved in a Christmas meal or the occasional evening out. If you run a larger office, coach trips to the theatre or even a weekend or week away somewhere can be arranged if the majority of staff are in agreement.

The big question to ask is whether your staff actually want to mix business with pleasure. Many people think that the two are best kept apart. You have probably heard the tales of 'staff only' Christmas parties causing havoc to otherwise happy marriages. Christmas is a time of goodwill and at a party many people tend to get a little too merry. Feeling happy and merry can then lead on to situations that are regretted the next day, but by that time it may be too late. Working relationships are often best kept at just that.

Perhaps the answer to staff outings being a success is to include partners and even families too. Family holidays, for instance, can be arranged far more cheaply if group bookings are made. In fact, nowadays the vast majority of staff outings do include the whole family, and there has been a definite move away from 'staff only' activities.

A word of warning if you are involved in organising a staff outing. Always ask for the money 'up front' otherwise you will find yourself let down at the last minute by people who have decided they would rather not go after all. Let them change their minds by all means, but if you cannot re-sell their place at least you have the money to pay for it. There is no reason why you should end up out of pocket.

CHECKLIST

● Do you work hard at keeping your staff happy?

● Do you have good training facilities?

● Have you got a sympathetic ear for problems?

● Do you hold regular staff appraisals?

● Are these positive rather than negative occasions?

● Are you prepared to sort out any trouble amongst your staff?

● Do you know how to discipline someone?

● Are you aware of the procedures to follow before dismissing a member of staff?

● Have you given any thought to arranging staff outings?

CASE STUDIES

Dorothy is understanding

Wendy, Dorothy's new part-timer, suddenly starts turning up late for work, obviously in an upset state. Dorothy lets this go on for a week or so, just in case it is a temporary phase, but things do not improve. One morning she tackles Wendy about it, and Wendy tells her that she has family problems. Apparently her husband is in danger of losing his job and they are both very worried about what they will do.

Dorothy listens as Wendy explains about their mortgage and all their other commitments. She knows that there is nothing she can do apart from sympathise, but she does tell Wendy that her husband was made redundant some years ago, and he managed to find himself another job, even though it was not as well paid as the one he had been used to. This does at least help Wendy to get matters into perspective in that other people have survived such upsets.

Dorothy asks Wendy to do her best to get in on time and to keep cheerful. She tells her to come and see her whenever she feels like a chat. This brings them closer together. Dorothy feels useful and no longer threatened by Wendy's high tech knowledge. Now they can begin to help each other.

Sue organises in-house training

Sue gets her cross-training courses under way. She intends all her temps to be trained on at least two Windows and Dos based word processing packages, plus two accounting packages. She arranges the courses for Saturday mornings and, by using her computer as well as the one in reception, she can take two temps at a time. She runs the training courses herself, as she has a good deal of experience. The girls come for a one month course at Sue's expense.

Stephen is heavy-handed

As he is under pressure to do so, Stephen sorts out a cheap word processing course for his typists to go on. He is amazed that after a couple of lessons they still do not know what they are doing!

Stephen has decided on monthly staff appraisals to begin with. At the first one he tells the typists and negotiators that he is far from satisfied with their efforts. He says they are all 'underperforming' and tells the negotiators that if they do not show some results soon they will be 'out'. He does not have a positive word to say to any of them.

Understandably, all the staff feel demoralised and angry. They just wish that they could have their old boss back again.

John gets it right

John plans an outing to the theatre for the staff and their partners. By making a large group booking the theatre and coach seats are very reasonable. Everyone has a great night out and a friendly atmosphere prevails, especially when John buys them all a drink afterwards as a 'thank you' for helping him out during his first weeks in a new job.

John's staff are well motivated and happy to work with their new boss.

POINTS FOR DISCUSSION

1. How important do you think it is to offer staff the opportunity to go on external training courses to learn about new office technology?

2. What would you do if a female member of your staff came and told you that she was being 'picked on' by one of the other women in the office?

3. Do you think it is necessary to arrange for staff to go on outings? Give four possible choices that would please all age groups.

7
Managing Office Paperwork

Even though in theory the amount of paper produced in an office should go down with increased use of electronic facilities, it does not seem to do so. We seem to like our 'bits of paper' to push around our desks, and indeed some organisations positively thrive on paper, every document being produced in duplicate or even triplicate.

In this chapter we will discuss:

- writing letters and memos
- taking and sending messages
- compiling reports
- preparing orders, invoices and statements
- designing and completing forms
- managing incoming mail
- managing outgoing mail
- setting up a manual filing system
- using an existing system
- retrieving information.

WRITING LETTERS AND MEMOS

The main difference between a letter and a memo, apart from the appearance, is that a letter is usually sent to someone outside an organisation whereas a memo is used for internal correspondence.

The planning and production is similar for either. You should:

- think about who you are writing to

- think about the purpose of the letter or memo

- decide whether it should be written in a formal or an informal way

79

● make a list of the points to be covered

● prepare a rough draft, starting a new paragraph for each new point

● make sure that your opening paragraph sets the scene and that your closing paragraph sums up the contents and any recommendations

● prepare a final copy of your letter or memo, amending the rough draft where necessary.

The layout of a business letter

Modern letters are produced using what is known as the **fully blocked layout** and **open punctuation**, which means that every line begins at the left margin and no punctuation is used except in the main body of the letter. It is very important to make sure that your letter is well displayed, accurate and free from any errors, to give a good impression of the company or organisation you are representing.

An example of a typical business letter is shown in figure 12.

The numbers at the left hand side of the letter are explained as follows:

1. The company letterhead.
2. References. 'Your Ref' is only inserted if previous correspondence on the same topic from the recipient shows a reference. References are usually the initials of the sender and of the typist. Sometimes a file reference is added.
3. Date. Do not put 'th', 'st', or 'rd' after the numbers.
4. Inside name and address. Use a separate line for each part of the recipient's name and address. The post town should be in capital letters.
5. The salutation or greeting.
6. Subject heading.
7. Main body of the letter, subdivided into paragraphs.
8. Complimentary close.
9. The name of the company sending the letter.
10. The name of the sender and his/her designation or position.
11. Enclosure mark, showing that something accompanies the letter.

The layout of a memo

Most memos are produced on company headed memo paper. Like a letter, the blocked layout with open punctuation should be used. They tend to be less formal than a business letter, however, because the people involved usually know each other. An example of a simple memo follows:

MEMORANDUM

To: Susan White
From: Theresa Amberley
Ref: TA/SW
Date: 13 July 19XX

Jones Brothers — Company Brochures
I can confirm that we now have the order for the above project and
I would like you to arrange production as soon as possible.

I have told Mr Brown that these brochures should be ready by the
end of July. If you can do them sooner, so much the better. They
want 500 to start with.

Please keep me informed

Fig. 11. A typical memo.

Taking copies

Normally a copy of a letter or memo is taken to keep in the files.

TAKING AND SENDING MESSAGES

Messages can be taken and sent in numerous different ways. Telephone
messages, face-to-face messages, written messages, faxed messages, are
all examples, and there are many more.

Taking a message

It is very important to take accurate messages. This means that all the
details should be noted down, rather than relying on memory. Many
organisations use some sort of message form. You may find the example on page 83 useful.

Make sure that all messages are passed on without delay. Keep a copy
of the message just in case there is a query later on.

1.
AMBERLEY SECRETARIAL SERVICES
25 The High Street
Bridmouth
Herts
SG21 9YH

Tel: 01992 768543

2. Our Ref: BYH/AFT
    Your Ref: CYJ/ANM

3. 12 July 19XX

4. Mr Colin Jones
    Jones Brothers Ltd
    43 Low Road
    BRIDMOUTH
    Herts
    SG12 8YN

5. Dear Mr Jones

6. **Company brochures**

    I am writing to confirm our conversation yesterday, when
    we agreed to supply you with 500 company brochures
    according to the agreed specification, a copy of which is
    enclosed.

7. These brochures should be ready by the end of this month,
    and I will telephone you immediately they are available.

    I would like to thank you for placing this valuable order
    with us and assure you of our best attention at all times.

8. Yours sincerely
9. AMBERLEY SECRETARIAL SERVICES

10. Theresa Amberley
    MANAGING DIRECTOR

11. enc

Fig. 12. A standard business letter.

MESSAGE FORM

MESSAGE FOR ....

DATE ....TIME ....

MESSAGE RECEIVED FROM...

OF ....

THEIR TELEPHONE NUMBER..

MESSAGE TAKEN BY ....

MESSAGE READS ....

....

....

....

....

ACTION REQUIRED ....

Fig. 13. A message form.

Sending a message

If you need to send a message this can be handwritten or typed depending on the time available and the formality required. A handwritten message, although quicker, is not suitable if the message needs to be formally recorded. Very formal messages will normally be transmitted in the form of a memo.

COMPILING REPORTS

The purpose of a report is to pass on information. In office life reports are many and varied, covering everything from 'the usefulness of the paperclip' to 'the future of the company'!

Planning

It is important to ask a few questions before beginning your report:

● What do you hope to achieve?
● Who is going to read it?

- How will you obtain the necessary information?
- How will you present the report?
- Should you use technical or non-technical language?

When you have answered these questions you can begin structuring your report.

Structuring

The structure of most reports is as follows:

- the title

- the introduction — explaining the purpose of the report

- the main body — where all the relevant information is set out clearly in paragraphs

- the conclusion and any recommendations

- acknowledgements — if a person or a reference book has helped you to write your report then you should say so at the end.

- appendices — for any additional information.

Here is a summary for good report writing:

1. Decide on the main aim of the report.
2. Gather together all relevant information.
3. Sort this information out into logical order.
4. Prepare a first draft of the report.
5. Amend where necessary.
6. Prepare a final copy of the report.
7. Remember to mention any outside sources of information.
8. Circulate your report as appropriate.

PREPARING ORDERS, INVOICES AND STATEMENTS

It is very likely that within your office environment you will be involved in producing business documents. Either these can be prepared and stored for use on the computer or else pre-printed forms can be utilised. The most common documents are:

Enquiry
The buyer will ask the seller for details of the goods available. This enquiry will normally be set out in letter form.

Quotation
The seller sends the necessary details, such as price, quantity, description of goods and date of supply to the buyer, either by letter or on a printed form which may include standard terms and conditions.

Order
If the buyer is satisfied with the quotation, he will place an order for the goods he requires, again either by letter or printed form.

Delivery note
When the goods are delivered the buyer will be asked by the driver to sign a copy of the delivery note to verify that the goods have been received.

Invoice
This is probably the most common business document of all. The seller sends a sales invoice to the buyer stating full details of the goods which have been delivered, including the amount of money due and the time given for payment.

Credit note
If any goods are returned, the supplier will issue a credit note to the buyer allowing him to use the value of this against future purchases.

Statement
Usually sent monthly or quarterly. Statements give full details of all transactions which have taken place and been invoiced during the statement period, and the amount now due for payment. Payment should be made when the statement reaches the buyer.

Value Added Tax
Rather like Income Tax and National Insurance, Value Added Tax (VAT) is very complicated and outside the realms of this book. To put it simply, traders with a turnover over a certain amount per annum must be registered for VAT. This means they usually have to charge their customers VAT on goods they sell, and pay this over to HM Customs and Excise. Theoretically the trader should be able to claim enough VAT

back from goods purchased, telephone bills, petrol and so on to break even, but in practice this does not always happen.

E & OE
The seller will often have 'E & OE' printed at the bottom of his business documents. This means 'errors and omissions excepted'. It protects the seller from any error that may have been made in the documentation. For example, if £10.00 appears on an invoice for a chair, when the sum should have been £100.00, then the seller is still within his rights to claim the full £100.00 from the buyer.

Business documents can be prepared in many different ways and each organisation will have its own way of setting them out. An example of an invoice is shown in figure 14.

DESIGNING AND COMPLETING FORMS

Forms have a variety of uses in the average office. For example, forms are used:

● for job applications
● to record statistics
● to record messages
● for standardised information to be inserted.

Design
When designing a form think about:

● the purpose of the form
● the type of person who will be using the form
● the information required
● the questions to be asked in order to gain that information
● the best layout to use
● the space required for the information to be inserted.

Completion
Completing a form needs thought and preparation. Read the form carefully, and make notes, so that you are confident about what you are going to put where. When you are satisfied with your notes, transfer the information onto your form. If you are filling in a form that contains 'dots' make sure that your typing or writing just clears those dots, otherwise the information will be difficult to read.

INVOICE

Invoice No: 1200   VAT Reg No 645 908 145

Better Banqueting
65 Bridge Road
Barstock
Middlesex
BN56 7XH

Date: 13 March 19XX

To: The Ship Hotel
                 Barstock
                 Middlesex
                 BA23 9XH

Your Order: 34
Terms: 30 days

Ref No	Quantity and Description	Price £	Total £
CH/36	50 Banqueting Chairs – Pink	70.00	3,500
TA/27	10 Oak Refectory Tables	90.00	900
	Sub Total	160.00	4,400
	VAT Total		770
	TOTAL		£5,170

E & OE

Fig. 14. An example of an invoice.

CAR PARKING PERMIT

Name ....

Address..

....

....

Department...

Office extension no. ....Home tel no ....

Date of application...

_____

Permit approved by ....

Date permit approved...

Date permit expires ....

Information to be inserted:
Name: Stephen Long
Address: 23 Ship Street, Bridgenorth, Herts SG19 8HB
Department: Sales
Office No: 2314 Home No: 01992 453123
Date: 12 August 19XX

Fig. 15. An example of a form and the information to be inserted.

CAR PARKING PERMIT

Name ....*Stephen Long*.............................

Address........*23 Ship Street*.............................

.............*Bridgenorth*....................................

............*Herts   SG 19   8HB*............................

Deparment ......*Sales*......................................

Office extension no.....*2314*.........Home tel no *01992 453123*

Date of application........*12 August 19XX*...............

_____

Permit approved by ....

Date permit approved...

Date permit expires ....

Fig. 16. An example of the completed form.

An example of a form is shown in figure 15 and the completed version follows in figure 16.

MANAGING INCOMING MAIL

When mail is received it is important to deal with it quickly and effectively. In large organisations a separate mail room may handle all incoming and outgoing mail. In smaller offices, however, the manager and his or her staff will be responsible for mail handling.

When dealing with incoming mail remember:

● All personal and confidential mail should only be opened by the person to whom it is addressed.

● All mail received should be date stamped.

● Where enclosures are mentioned, check to see that they have arrived with the correspondence.

● Clip any enclosures to the correspondence.

● Enter up money received in a remittances book.

● Take action, or instruct others to take action, on all incoming mail just as soon as possible.

MANAGING OUTGOING MAIL

Routine outgoing mail should be ready for posting by mid-afternoon, leaving time for any emergency correspondence to be dealt with if necessary. If letters or packets are to be sent by recorded delivery or registered post, they must be kept separate as they will need to be taken into the Post Office rather than dropped into the nearest post box.

Before posting you should check that:

● Any enclosures have been enclosed.

● Letters or other correspondence are error free and accurate in content.

● Appropriate envelopes are being used. Many organisations use window envelopes for routine letters.

● Envelopes have been either stamped or franked correctly.

SETTING UP A MANUAL FILING SYSTEM

A manual filing system involves storing paper in filing cabinets, folders, shelves or boxes. When setting up any filing system bear in mind that it needs to be:

● quick and simple to operate

● suitable for the information to be placed in it

● capable of expansion

● capable of safeguarding documents including confidential material.

Assuming that the filing system is to operate within your office, you will need to consider how to store your files and what storage equipment you will need.

Vertical or lateral filing

The vertical method is the most popular method of filing. Metal filing cabinets are usually used and the files are suspended in an upright position in each drawer. The file contents are listed on thin strips which are placed on the top edge of each file. Because the files are stored in cabinets they are kept clean, and can also be locked away if necessary.

With lateral filing the files are suspended from rails in horizontal rows on racks or shelves, rather like books on a bookshelf. This is a useful way of storing files if your office has alcoves or room for shelves to be easily incorporated. If space is limited the shelves can be built right up to the ceiling, so long as a good pair of steps is close at hand! Although shelves are cheaper than filing cabinets, files do not keep as clean as they do in filing cabinets.

Alphabetical or numerical filing

Having decided what to store your files in, you then need to consider whether to file them alphabetically or by number.

Alphabetical filing is quick and simple to operate. Files are placed in alphabetical order according to organisation name or, if there is no organisation name, by individual name.

With numerical filing, each file is given a number and filed in the appropriate number order. Often this system incorporates an index where an alphabetical list is kept too, in case the number of the file is not known.

Although the numerical system is capable of greater expansion than the alphabetical system, it is more complicated to operate, particularly if a separate index is kept.

USING AN EXISTING SYSTEM

Using someone else's filing system is never easy. You will need to take time to familiarise yourself with how the system works. In time you may make changes, particularly if you decide that the files are not being stored in the most effective way. There are, however, basic filing rules that will help you to cope with any filing system:

● Make sure that everything to be filed has been finished with.

● Sort the documents into order before beginning to file.

● Place the documents carefully in the file, in the correct order — usually date order.

● Make sure that the documents are being filed in the **right** file.

● Remove paper clips before filing. Staple if necessary.

● Keep filing cabinets locked at night.

● Keep the filing up to date. Filing is a job that everyone hates but it has to be done.

RETRIEVING INFORMATION

The true test of an efficient filing system is when information needs to be retrieved. If it can be found easily the filing system is a success.

Everyone operating the system should be told how to do so properly. For instance, if information from a file is needed, make sure an 'Absent Card' is filled in before that file is removed. On this card the date taken, the file number or name and the name of the person who removed it should be recorded. When the file is returned the return date should be filled in too. If everyone respects the system files will always be easily accessible.

Of course, not all information needed in an office is kept in a manual filing system. Information can also be accessed from your own computerised systems (see Chapter 8), and from outside electronic databases such as Ceefax, Prestel and Oracle.

It is a good idea to keep several reference books in the office too: The most useful ones include:

- a dictionary and thesaurus
- an encyclopedia
- Royal Mail guides
- telephone directories and *Yellow Pages*
- maps and travel information.

CHECKLIST FOR OFFICE PAPERWORK

- Do you know how to present an effective business letter and memo?

- Can you prepare a message form suitable for your organisation?

- Are you aware of the importance of good planning for a well written report?

- Can you design and complete forms easily and quickly?

- Are you able to handle incoming and outgoing mail?

- Do you know the difference between vertical and lateral filing?

- Would you be able to choose between an alphabetical and a numerical filing system?

- Do you know the basic rules for filing?

- Can you find files easily in your filing system?

- Do you know what to do when you remove a file?

- Are you aware of the various reference books available?

CASE STUDIES

Dorothy designs a message form

Dorothy and her staff often have to take messages for the teachers. She is fed up with having to chase around the school looking for them, and so she decides to design a message form for non-urgent messages, which can be pushed into their pigeon hole. She sends out a copy of this form, which is similar to the form in figure 13, and a covering memo as follows:

MEMORANDUM
From: Dorothy Stringer
To: All teaching staff
Date: 12 September 19XX

MESSAGES
You will no doubt be aware that the office staff frequently take messages for many of you during the working day. Lately we have been spending a considerable amount of time looking for individual teachers to pass on what are often non-urgent messages.

You will find enclosed a copy of a new Message Form that I am introducing for all non-urgent messages. This will be completed and placed in your pigeon holes for you to collect. All urgent messages will continue to be relayed to you immediately.

Your co-operation will be much appreciated.

enc

Sue designs an application form

Sue recruited all her first temps from their CVs and letter of application. Now that her business is gradually expanding she decides to use an application form instead. After giving the matter thought she comes up with the simple form in figure 17.

Stephen makes his feelings clear

After three months in his new job Stephen has to prepare a report for his head office in London. He decides to divide the report into three sections: Staff, Office Performance and The Future. He is particularly articulate on paper and head office will be under no illusions when they read his report.

Application Form

Surname ....First names ....

Address ....

....

Tel no ....Date of birth ....

Qualifications ....

....

....

....

....

Working experience: (list most recent employer first with
position held and list of duties. Then list other employers with
title of jobs only)

....

....

....

....

....

....

Have you ever worked as a temp before? ....

Could you start work immediately? ....

Please provide the telephone number of someone who would
give you a reference ....

Signed...Date ....

Fig. 17. A simple application form.

Report on Goddards Estate Agency, Shirehill, Suffolk
June — September 19XX

Staff
Staff relations have been anything but successful during the three months. Mr Baines, my predecessor, seemed to adopt a very lax attitude and I am having to put this right. The introduction of word processing packages for the two typists did not meet with their approval. I have sent them both on a course to learn how to use them, giving them an ultimatum that otherwise they will be out of a job.

Office performance
In line with the rest of the country this has been a very quiet period. Prices continue to fall slightly and confidence in the market does not seem to have been restored. We do have demand for cottages, particularly in the £60,000 to £80,000 price range, and for first-time buyers' houses in the £30,000 to £40,000 bracket. Estate houses are proving very difficult to sell.

The future
I am determined to bring this office up to date. At the moment we are underperforming and I have told the staff so. During the next few months entire redecoration and re-equipping will take place. I just hope this inspires my staff to work in a more modern way. If not, drastic measures might have to be taken.

This report, although ruthless and unfeeling in content, will leave head office in no doubt about Stephen's intentions!

John drafts an apology
John has the unpleasant task of writing a letter to a patient whose notes got mixed up at their last clinic appointment.

John's rough jottings
Write to Mr C Smith, 23 Old Road, Rochford, Sussex BN23 8YH
Apologise for mix up at Dr Rahl's clinic.
His notes now available and made up to date.
Say it won't happen again.

Final letter on hospital headed paper

23 September 19XX

Mr C Smith
23 Old Road
ROCHFORD
Sussex
BN23 8YH

Dear Mr Smith

I am writing to apologise sincerely for the mix up with your notes when you attended Dr Rahl's clinic the other day. Apparently we have two Mr Cyril Smiths and the wrong notes were selected by my staff.

We have made sure that your notes are now fully up to date and have marked them with a special coded sticker to show that you attend Dr Rahl's clinic. This will ensure that no similar mishaps arise in the future.

Plans are in hand for a completely re-vamped Outpatients Department to be opened soon. At that time all the notes will be computerised and instantly accessible on screen. Until then I hope you will accept my assurance that I will personally make sure that you are not inconvenienced in any way when you come to see us again.

Yours sincerely

John Wray
Outpatient Administrator

POINTS FOR DISCUSSION

1. How important do you think it is for a letter to be well presented and error free? Give reasons.

2. What are the essential points to remember when setting up a new manual filing system?

3. List the advantages and disadvantages of written communication compared with oral or spoken communication.

8
The Electronic Office

As we said in the first chapter of this book, the office of today is vastly different from that of even a few years ago. In fact, at the moment, every year that passes appears to mark yet another revolutionary advance in technology.

In this chapter we will discuss:

- working in the electronic office
- handling telephone calls
- sending fax and telex messages
- how computers and word processing programs work
- using a spreadsheet
- using electronic mail
- using microfilm and electronic filing systems
- complying with the Data Protection Act
- teleworking
- telecottages

WORKING IN THE ELECTRONIC OFFICE

Managing an electronic office is in some ways harder than managing the old fashioned type of office and in other ways easier. It is unlikely that you will have the same number of staff to manage as in a similar office, say, ten years ago. That should cut down the number of staff problems to deal with and staff wages to pay.

On the other hand, as we have said before, modern technology will only work effectively if the people operating it are properly trained. It will be your job to make sure that first you know how to make best use of the technology available to you, and that secondly your staff receive adequate training.

You must have been into the bank or library only to be told that 'the computer is down so we can't check your balance/order you a book' etc.

In fact computers and computerised systems are blamed for a great number of communication breakdowns and not all of them are the machines' fault.

Working in the electronic office can be very exciting, but no one should underestimate the importance of understanding the systems involved and of being able to use those systems efficiently.

HANDLING TELEPHONE CALLS

Telephone systems along with everything else have also become very sophisticated over the last few years. No longer do switchboard operators sit all day putting plugs in and out of a switchboard. Today's switchboards can do remarkable things almost all on their own! In fact in most small offices there is no need for a switchboard operator at all because calls can be answered by any extension and all extensions can make outside calls.

However sophisticated the equipment has become it should be remembered that the basic telephone skills are the same as they have ever been. When you make or receive a call you are responsible for giving a good impression of the company or organisation you represent.

Making a call

- Always be polite.
- Always be brief.
- Say who you are and who you represent.
- Make notes as the conversation progresses.
- Speak clearly and slowly.
- Repeat difficult words.
- Use everyday language.

It is very common to be subjected to music playing via the switchboard whilst you are being connected. Try not to get impatient, even if it does seem that the operator is waiting for the song to end before putting you through!

Receiving a call

The same guidelines as above apply, plus a few extras:

- Answer the telephone stating the company name, your name and any department or extension number.

- Try to help the caller, whether or not the call is actually meant for you.

- If you need to transfer the caller, say what you are going to do. Never leave the caller with a 'dead' line and no knowledge of what is going on.

- If the person the caller wishes to speak to is not available either ask the caller to ring again, take their number and pass it on to the person concerned, or take a message.

Whether making or receiving telephone calls, perhaps the two most important points to always remember are:

- to be polite

- to keep paper and pencil nearby for note taking. Never rely on memory. Twenty 'phone conversations in one morning can tend to dull the brain!

Using telephone answering machines

Telephone answering machines come in three main guises. They can be an answering machine alone, or a combined telephone/answering machine, or a fax, telephone and answering machine all in one.

The idea of an answering machine is for calls to be recorded whilst you are away from the office. This can save valuable business being lost because you are not personally available to take the calls. Most machines use a small cassette tape, although a few are now fully digitalised and therefore 'tapeless'. When a call is made, the caller listens firstly to your pre-recorded message and then leaves his or her message on the machine for you to access on your return.

No one seems to like talking to an answering machine, but they are becoming more and more necessary with the increased number of small businesses being run from offices which are not continually manned.

SENDING FAX AND TELEX MESSAGES

Telex or teleprinter machines have been around for over 60 years. Fax machines are much more recent. A fax machine produces an exact copy of a message or document, rather like a photocopy, whereas a telex message is usually typed at the same time as being transmitted.

Using a fax machine

Sending a fax is faster than sending a telex and a fax machine, unlike a telex, can be used to reproduce diagrams and pictures. The cost is the same as a telephone call, which is cheaper than sending a telex. Recently produced fax machines can incorporate a telephone, answerphone and a copier facility.

Using a fax machine is very simple. You place your message or document in the tray of your machine. You then dial the recipient's fax number and the recipient's machine reproduces a facsimile of the original. A disadvantage, however, is that the quality of reproduction is not always good, particularly if the machine uses thermal paper. Some of the recent machines are now using plain paper, which gives a much clearer copy.

Fax machines are cheap to buy and even small businesses can afford to buy one. You can connect your fax to a computer via a modem, which can then dial any fax machine, identify itself as being a fax and send information over to the recipient.

Using a telex machine

A modern telex machine consists of a VDU (screen), keyboard, printer and often a word processing facility for preparing and editing text. On the latest machines there is no need to dial. Calls can be selected from the keyboard. Other features can include:

- facility to hold incoming messages in the memory and then re-transmit them

- ability to repeat same message to several different destinations and even to translate into different languages

- storage in the memory for the most commonly used telex numbers

- facility to link computers throughout an organisation to the telex machines so that messages can be transmitted direct from those computers.

The telex system is more complicated and more sophisticated than the simple fax machine. In large organisations both have their place, but for the smaller office user a fax machine will probably prove to be a better investment.

HOW COMPUTERS AND WORD PROCESSING PROGRAMS WORK

Thousands upon thousands of books have been written on every conceivable computer system and every possible word processing package. If you are faced with a new system or package then, you would do well to select one of these books to read.

For our purposes, however, we will just take a look at the very basics:

Computers

Computers process information using **software** and instructions from a **keyboard** or a **mouse**. Software is a set of electronic instructions which enable computers to carry out their functions. The information processing takes place in the central processing unit (CPU) of computers. Apart from the CPU, which usually looks like a box, computers also have a **monitor** or visual display unit (VDU) and a keyboard. They can have a printer and other devices attached too. All the physical components of computers are known as **hardware**.

The software and other data can be stored either on a **hard disk**, which is an integral part of the CPU, or on a removable **floppy disk** or diskette.

A computer can operate independently or it can be linked electronically with other computers to form a **network**. A local area network (LAN) covers a small area such as an office building. A wide area network (WAN) covers a much larger area.

Many offices have what is called a **mainframe** computer. This large computer can be electronically linked to small desktop personal computers (PCs). This enables them to use the information stored on the big computer and to communicate with each other.

Word processing programs

Almost every office will have a computer and a word processing program as software to use on that computer. There are hundreds of different word processing programs and each one has its merits and individual features.

Word processing, as its name suggests, actually means the processing of words. Most simple word processing programs allow the operator to:

- correct text
- delete or add text

- store text
- centre text
- justify text
- rearrange text
- spellcheck text
- add headers and footers to text
- display text in columns
- change line spacing and pitch size
- merge names and addresses with standard letters.

There is no need for any text to be printed out until the operator is satisfied that it is perfect. Once it is ready, as many copies as necessary can be printed out an then the document can be filed away, on disk, for future reference.

The packages available have revolutionised the office world of today. Secretaries of the past are becoming administrators/PAs of the future, their straightforward typing duties taking up only a part of their day, because of the ease with which documents can now be produced. Indeed, some organisations are doing without typing pools and secretaries altogether, their personnel preferring to prepare their own correspondence.

USING A SPREADSHEET

Day-to-day office accounts can be very easily programmed, updated and logged by using one of the spreadsheet programs currently on the market for use with a computer.

In a simplified form, a spreadsheet is a table of numbers arranged in columns. These numbers can be changed and arithmetical calculations can be automatically carried out. Spreadsheet programs can also convert tabular material into a chart to give a more visual image.

It is best to choose one of the well known packages, and do check to see that your computer will run it efficiently before making your purchase.

Figure 18 is an example of a very simple spreadsheet.

There are many advantages of using a computer rather than pencil and paper for accounts work. These include:

- speed

- accuracy

The Ship Hotel

Bar sales during 19XX

	Spirits £	Beers £	Soft Drinks £
West Bar	50 000	40 000	30 000
East Bar	80 000	45 000	55 000
North Bar	30 000	65 000	40 000

These figures can then be totalled:

Bar sales during 19XX

	Spirits £	Beers £	Soft Drinks £
West Bar	50 000	40 000	30 000
East Bar	80 000	45 000	55 000
North Bar	30 000	65 000	40 000
TOTALS	160 000	150 000	125 000

Fig. 18. A simple spreadsheet.

● ease of alteration

● automatic creation of charts

● lower cost in the long term, compared with labour hours necessary to constantly alter and revise figures on paper.

USING ELECTRONIC MAIL

Electronic mail in one form or another is here to stay. Indeed the modern day telex and fax are both forms of electronic mail.

Another, and very popular, type of electronic mail is known as the British Telecom Gold EMail Service. This service enables customers to send electronic mail messages from one computer to another both in this country and abroad using BT's telephone network and relay computers.

Electronic mail is very important for the business user today. Time differences between one country and another can be forgotten. Postage delays can be forgotten. Every urgent message can reach its destination almost immediately. The possibilities are endless and, who knows, perhaps in years to come electronic mail will not only be available in all of our offices but in most of our homes too.

USING MICROFILM AND ELECTRONIC FILING SYSTEMS

The problem with manual filing systems is that they take up a lot of space in what is often a small office. They way to avoid this 'paper mountain' is to store information either by microfilming or on a computer storage medium.

Microfilming
Microfilming is the filing of documents that have been photographed, developed on film in greatly reduced size and printed on plastic strips or cards. An A4 sheet of information can be reduced to a minute size. If the document needs to be looked at, a viewfinder is used to enlarge the image on the screen. If a paper copy is required, the enlarged image can be reproduced.

Electronic computer filing
Electronic systems of filing, such as word processors and computers, enable documents to be filed on a computer storage medium. There are many different ways of storing information on computers. These include using:

- A **floppy disk**. A floppy disk is portable which means that it is removed from the machine when not in use and has to be re-inserted to call up files on it.

- A **hard disk**. A hard disk is the computer's built-in storage facility. Files on a hard disk can be accessed at any time.

COMPLYING WITH THE DATA PROTECTION ACT

With so much information being stored and accessed, from computer to computer and from country to country, there is always a danger that some of this information will fall into the wrong hands. The Data Protection Act 1984 was introduced to try to minimise this danger in so far as people are concerned. The legislation covers all personal information stored on any public computer system, other than information kept by the police or the Inland Revenue.

Under the conditions of the Act, all organisations storing information concerning the general public must register with a central registrar, stating exactly what information they hold and what they intend to use it for. They are also under an obligation to keep this information accurate, up-to-date and confidential. Members of the public are entitled to look at their own personal information whenever they wish.

Much has been written about 'Big Brother' watching over us and knowing our every move in life. The Data Protection Act helps, but as more and more information becomes available to more and more people it may be that stronger measures will be necessary to protect everyone's right to privacy.

TELEWORKING

Teleworking, or 'electronic homeworking' as it is sometimes known, has become more and more popular over the last few years. The idea in its simplest form is that employees work from their own home rather than in a traditional office. They do their work using a computer and often other equipment too, and they are linked electronically to their head office. They will probably need to visit that head office only on rare occasions.

Working from home conjures up a picture of someone sitting in their country cottage looking out over lush green fields with birds twittering in the background. In theory, no commuting to and from work and peace and quiet rather than the continual 'buzz' of a modern open plan office sounds like a really 'stress free' way to spend your life. In practice, however, these home offices are often in cities rather than in the country and you have to be the right kind of person to cope with the feelings of solitude and loneliness that teleworking can impose.

The term 'teleworking' can also be said to extend to remote 'call centres' where many people are grouped together handling customer telephone calls for large organisations such as mail order companies and banks. These offices are manned 24 hours a day in remote areas of the country, admittedly providing company for the teleworkers, but few other benefits. From the employer's point of view, however, they provide the opportunity to operate with lower rents and wages than in the big cities.

With business rents and rates continuing to increase and purse strings tightening, it is inevitable that the number of teleworkers in some form will continue to rise, but perhaps not to the extent that was thought at first. Many managers tend to be very wary about controlling an 'absent workforce' and prefer their employees to be in the office where they can keep an eye on them. Also, some of the teleworkers themselves may begin to rebel, preferring to work with other people in a 'normal' office.

Teleworking suits some people very well and many teleworkers say that they would never want to return to the traditional way of office working. What is not so certain however, is what percentage of the total workforce will ever be employed in such a way, partly because of the hesitance of many organisations to adopt such a scheme, and partly because of the reluctance of many workers to combine their office and personal life under one roof.

TELECOTTAGES

The first telecottage was started in Scandinavia in the 1980s. It was originally designed to be a computer based information centre set in a rural community, with the aim of providing training and information resources to that community that would not otherwise be available. The first British telecottage opened in 1989, with similar aims in mind, and the number has grown steadily ever since.

Broadly speaking most telecottages offer:

● public access to a wide range of 'high tech' equipment including computers

● training facilities to help local people acquire business skills

● services to assist other business users.

Every telecottage works individually and is either home or, more often, office based. A considerable number are funded by the Training and Enterprise Councils (TECs) in England and Wales and the Local Enterprise Companies (LECs) in Scotland. EU funding is sometimes available too. Since their humble beginnings, many have grown very large and offer a wide variety of services apart from the training. These can include:

● word processing
● desk top publishing
● CV preparation
● spreadsheets and accounts
● message handling
● reporting facilities
● translation service

- mail shots
- leaflet production
- thesis and book preparation.

The Telecottage Association, which was formed in 1993, already has several thousand members, and further information on what telecottages are all about can be obtained from them (Tel: 01453 836174).

CHECKLIST

- Are you well prepared for the electronic office?

- Do you give a good impression when you use the telephone?

- Are you familiar with fax and telex?

- Do you understand the importance of electronic mail?

- Have you considered the possibility of electronic rather than paper filing systems?

- Are you aware of the Data Protection Act and who it sets out to protect?

- Do you understand the parts of a computer?

- Are you familiar with any word processing packages?

- Have you fully understood the implications of teleworking and telecottages?

CASE STUDIES

Dorothy embraces new technology
Miss Porter, the headmistress, has been telling Dorothy for years that the school needs a fax machine, but Dorothy has thought up all sorts of excuses to avoid getting one.

Now Wendy has managed to persuade Dorothy that it really would be a good idea. She takes Dorothy to a friend's office and shows her how it works. Seeing that it is not as complicated as she had feared, Dorothy agrees and they have one installed in the school office.

After a month Dorothy cannot imagine how they ever managed without a fax. They often have to send messages to other schools in the area and with a fax she finds the job is halved. No more tedious letters and envelopes to prepare. In fact Dorothy starts inventing reasons to send faxes to people and her excitement over her new 'toy' makes Wendy smile to herself!

Sue uses her computer storage facility

Sue decides to store all her temp staff details together with details of the companies she deals with on her computer. It takes her some time to input all the information, but once she has done so she is able to get rid of all the bits of paper that she has accumulated over the past months. Using a computerised filing system suits her business well, because information can be accessed and updated as circumstances dictate.

Stephen overdoes it

During one of his many mad moments, Stephen decides that his negotiators are not answering the telephone as he thinks they should. He writes them out a speech to learn, and tells them they must say it every time they answer the 'phone in future. The speech he gives them is as follows:

Good morning/Good afternoon, this is Goddards Estate Agency. My name is . . . . I am a negotiator, trained to give you expert advice on your buying and selling requirements. You will find our company ready and willing to cater for all your needs. Now, how may I help you?

The negotiators try the speech but find people hang up on them because they think they are talking to an answering machine. Needless to say, by the end of the first week, they refuse to use this 'blurb' any more!

John

John sets out several standard letters for one of his girls to input to the computer system. He feels it will save time if they can be called up and completed as required and then sent out to the appropriate people. His letter for attending the Outpatients Clinics is as follows:

Put on hospital headed paper

Our Ref
Date
Name and Address

Dear
An appointment has been made for you to attend ....
...................................Clinic on ....
at ....in the Outpatient Department.

Would you please bring this letter with you and report to the Reception Desk at the front of the Outpatient Department.

If this appointment is inconvenient for you please let us know as soon as possible.

Yours sincerely

John Wray
Outpatient Administrator

POINTS FOR DISCUSSION

1. Do you think the modern office is easier or harder to work in than the office of, say, ten years ago?

2. Can you list six advantages of electronic rather than manual filing methods?

3. What is your opinion of teleworking? Do you think it has a viable future?

9
Greetings and Meetings

Dealing with people successfully, particularly people outside your office environment, is a skill that needs to be practised.

In this chapter we will discuss:

- keeping an office diary
- organising a reception area
- welcoming visitors
- offering hospitality
- dealing with unwelcome visitors
- planning informal meetings
- getting the best out of meetings
- arranging a formal meeting
- chairing a meeting.

KEEPING AN OFFICE DIARY

If you are to run your office efficiently you must know where you and any of your colleagues are going to be at a given time. That means keeping a note of all appointments, meetings, days off, holidays etc.

An office diary can either be stored on computer, where information can be accessed and updated daily, or a traditional paper diary can be kept. Whichever method you choose, it is a good idea for you to carry a small pocket diary around with you too, as a double-check when you are away from the office. Make sure that both diaries are kept up to date.

If other people are involved in making appointments for you ensure that they know when you are available. Similarly, tell other office members where you are going if you have to leave the office. They cannot be expected to cover for you if you do not keep them informed of your whereabouts.

It is a good idea to incorporate 'memory joggers' into your diary. For instance, birthdays, important occasions, following up an ongoing business matter, can all be recorded under the appropriate days.

If your organisation has a separate reception, with a receptionist, make sure that he or she is informed of your appointments and movements for each day too.

The most important points to remember about an office diary are to:

- keep the diary up to date
- make sure enough time is allowed for travelling between outside appointments
- leave spare time at the beginning and end of the day for emergencies etc
- write clearly and concisely when using a traditional paper diary
- keep a pocket diary too.

ORGANISING A RECEPTION AREA

Your office may or may not have a separate reception area, but for our purposes we will assume that you are involved in setting up a reception area in a room separate from your office.

As the reception area is usually the first place that a visitor sees, it is important to make sure it looks welcoming and gives a good impression of your organisation. The receptionist too should look pleasant, well groomed and generally pleased to see whoever has arrived.

Pastel colours on the walls, a decent carpet on the floor, and an efficient heating and air conditioning system, will all help to give the desired effect. Apart from the furniture, extra touches such as pictures, plants, subtle lighting, perhaps even a tropical fish tank, will enhance that effect still further.

Basic fixtures and fittings
- comfortable chairs for visitors
- an upright chair for anyone who cannot easily get out of a comfortable chair
- a coffee table or round table for the middle of the room
- a reception desk and typist chair
- a telephone switchboard, or telephone
- good reference books and internal/external telephone directories
- coat rack
- wastepaper bin/s
- a vending machine if other refreshment facilities are not available
- a selection of newspapers and magazines
- information about your organisation.

Depending on the receptionist's other duties, other equipment could well be necessary too, including:

- a computer, possibly with printer
- a fax machine
- a photocopier.

Exactly how the furniture and other items are arranged will depend on the size of the room and who is going to be using it. Just so long as the overall effect is of a well furnished, attractively decorated, clean and tidy room, with welcoming staff, your reception will provide the right 'image' for your visitors.

WELCOMING VISITORS

We have already touched on this under the previous heading. Not all visitors will, however, enter a reception area. Some will be invited straight into your office. Others will meet you at a pre-arranged outside venue.

Wherever visitors are received, it should be your aim to make them feel welcome and comfortable. First impressions count for a lot and welcome visitors are far more likely to make future clients or customers than visitors who are made to feel in the way and an inconvenience.

Show that you know your job. Prepare well in advance for visitors. Collect relevant files and information and make sure that you have everything to hand that you will need for the visit. Remember that everything relates to creating a good impression, both of yourself and of the company or organisation you represent.

OFFERING HOSPITALITY

Any visitor should be offered at least a cup of tea or coffee. It is always better if this is made by hand rather than by a vending machine, but the offer is the most important thing. Your visitor may have travelled some distance, and providing basic refreshments is the least you can do.

Hospitality can, of course, extend to business lunches and entertaining outside the office. Many organisations have cut down on this in recent years in an effort to cut costs. What used to be a good meal at a highly regarded restaurant is often reduced to a snack lunch at the local pub. If you run your own business it is up to you to decide how much you can afford to spend on entertaining. Be selective and tough. Only entertain people who are likely to pay you back in terms of business in the future.

Many managers in the past spent a good part of their working week entertaining, either at the pub, on the golf course, or at a restaurant. In fact it is a wonder that some of them found time to do any managing at all! But those days are largely gone, and more and more managers are finding their spending budgets cut to an absolute minimum. Whether any loss of business has resulted from this curtailment of management activities is a debatable issue.

DEALING WITH UNWELCOME VISITORS

Some unwelcome visitors are known to be absolute 'pains'. Others will arrive unexpectedly and unknown, demanding to see someone who is not willing to see them. Let us take a look at two examples:

The visitor who has arrived without an appointment

Most visitors will arrive for a pre-arranged appointment, so they will be expected and prepared for. There will, however, always be some visitors who demand to be seen even though they have not made a prior appointment.

If the visitor wants to see you, it is up to you to decide whether or not you have the time to see them. If you do, then make the point that you do not normally see people without an appointment (so that they do not repeat the episode), but that as you have a little spare time today you are prepared to fit them in. Should you not have the time available, you will have to suggest politely that an appointment is made for another time.

It may well be that the visitor did not want to see you but one of your colleagues who is not available. If this is the case, then try to help in any way you can. Should the visitor only wish to see your colleague:

- offer an appointment for another occasion
- remember to give your colleague a note of what has happened
- apologise to the visitor for not being able to help them.

The visitor who turns nasty

It is an unfortunate fact that not everyone in this life behaves in a socially acceptable way. At some time or another it is therefore likely that you will have to deal with a **really** unwelcome visitor, and by that we mean not just someone without an appointment.

Should you ever be in a situation where a visitor is being rude and abusive to you:

- remain calm and polite

- try to defuse the situation by sensible talking

- never take any chances. If you are out of your depth ask for assistance

- as a last resort find a way to call security or the police and have your visitor forcibly removed.

Hopefully this situation will not occur too often in your working life, but it is as well to be prepared for all eventualities.

PLANNING INFORMAL MEETINGS

In order to manage an office efficiently it is inevitable that you will be involved in both formal and informal meetings. The dictionary definition of 'meeting' is 'people gathered together for discussion'. The term 'meeting' is, however, often abused and if you telephone someone who is not available you will often be told that he or she is 'in a meeting' when in fact the person in question has slipped out to the shops, or gone to make the coffee!

Whenever you decide to hold any meeting, always ask yourself first whether it is really necessary. Many meetings are held as an excuse for a glorified chat about life in general, and such meetings are unlikely to be productive. An informal meeting is not normally documented and for this reason alone, the matter in hand is often pushed to the back, whilst other more interesting topics, such as the summer holidays and the local golf club, are discussed.

To be successful, a meeting needs to have a definite purpose. When that purpose has been clearly defined, the people involved can be contacted and a day and time for the meeting to take place can be arranged.

GETTING THE BEST OUT OF MEETINGS

As a manager you will probably be involved in two kinds of meetings: those you attend and those you arrange. The same basic skills apply to both situations:

- You should show consideration and tolerance for others.

- You should speak clearly and use words that everyone will understand.

- You should speak at the appropriate time and not when someone else is speaking.

- You should express your ideas in an easy to follow manner.

- You should listen carefully to other people's ideas.

- You should aim to feel part of your 'team'.

ARRANGING A FORMAL MEETING

A formal meeting is normally presided over by a chairperson. The meeting will be documented before, during and after it takes place. It may be a committee meeting, an annual general meeting for shareholders or just a company meeting. Some meetings are more formal than others. For example, an annual general meeting is usually very formal, whereas a meeting arranged to discuss the staff Christmas party is likely to be less so.

Before a formal meeting takes place a **notice of meeting** is sent out to those entitled to attend. This contains details of the date, time and place where the meeting is to be held. Nowadays, the notice of meeting is often combined with the **agenda**, which is a programme of the items to be discussed.

On the day of the meeting the Secretary, or other person appointed, takes notes known as the **minutes** of the meeting. These are taken down as the meeting progresses. They are not meant to be verbatim (word for word), but should contain:

- all relevant points discussed
- all resolutions
- all recommendations.

After the meeting these notes will be prepared in draft form for the chairperson to amend and then a final copy will be produced.

Examples of a combined notice and agenda and minutes of a meeting are shown in figures 19 and 20.

Terms used at meetings
There are certain standard terms that are used at more formal meetings. The most commonly used ones are listed below:
Abstain To refrain from voting.

ROSEDEAN HEALTH AND FITNESS CLUB

A meeting of the Committee will be held in the Gymnasium on Saturday 15 March 19XX at 1400 hrs.

AGENDA

1. Apologies for absence

2. Minutes of last meeting

3. Matters arising out of the minutes

4. Proposed covered swimming pool

5. Easter Sports Day

6. Any other business

7. Date of next meeting

Susan Roberts

Club Secretary

13 February 19XX

Fig. 19. Combined notice and agenda.

ROSEDEAN HEALTH AND FITNESS CLUB

Minutes of the meeting of the Committee held in the Gymnasium on Saturday 15 March 19XX at 1400 hrs.

Present
Sandy Johnson (Chairperson)
Susan Roberts (Secretary)
John Smythe
Richard Green
April Stevens
Polly Tucker
Martin Druid

Apologies for absence	Everyone was present at the meeting.
Minutes of last meeting	The minutes of the meeting on 1 February were read and approved as a correct record.
Matters arising out of the minutes	There were no matters arising out of the minutes.
Proposed covered swimming pool	John Smythe reported that the council had just given their permission for this project to go ahead. It was expected that work would begin within the next two weeks and would be completed by the beginning of August.
Easter sports day	Polly Tucker reported that plans for this annual event were well under way. It was proposed that Sir Cyril Plant should be approached with regard to presenting the prizes. If he was not available, Richard Green said that he would see if his father could stand in.
Any other business	There was no other business.
Date of next meeting	It was agreed that the date of the next meeting would be 21 April 19XX.

Fig. 20. Minutes of a meeting.

Ad hoc This usually refers to a committee specially appointed to carry out a specific task.

Address the chair This means that those wishing to speak must do so by speaking to the person in the chair, *ie* the chairperson, rather than carrying on conversations between themselves.

Adjournment A decision taken to adjourn the meeting, for example, to take a lunch break.

Amendment This is a proposal to alter a motion. It must be proposed, seconded and voted on before a decision is taken.

Any other business This time in a meeting gives an opportunity for those present to discuss items other than those listed under separate headings. It is often abbreviated to AOB.

Ballot Method of voting by means of a voting paper.

Carried A motion that has been agreed.

Casting vote If voting on a motion is equal, the chairperson may have the power to cast his or her vote, thus making the final decision.

Committee A group of people who meet to make decisions on behalf of an organisation.

Delegate A person representing a group of people and giving their views.

In camera A meeting in private, not open to the public.

Lie on the table When a document is not to be acted on it is said to 'lie on the table'.

Majority This means the number of votes necessary to carry a motion.

Motion A proposal put forward at a meeting is known as a motion. When a motion is put forward it is known as a **question**. If it is passed it is known as a **resolution**. It is usually necessary to propose and second a motion before it can be discussed.

No confidence Should those present at a meeting be unhappy with the actions of their chairperson, they can take a vote of 'no confidence'. If this is passed, the chairperson must vacate the chair in favour of someone else.

Postponement This is the action taken to postpone a meeting to a later date.

Proxy vote A person who cannot attend a meeting can ask someone else to vote on his or her behalf. This person is known as a proxy and the vote is a proxy vote.

Quorum With most formal meetings a minimum number of people must be present before the meeting can take place. This number is known as a quorum.

Resolution A motion passed at a meeting.

Unanimous A decision taken with the approval of everyone at the meeting.

CHAIRING A MEETING

A meeting will often succeed or fail because of the actions of one person — namely the chairperson. If you are involved in chairing a meeting, remember the following:

● Aim to make the meeting interesting and positive, not dull and boring.

● Define the objectives of the meeting.

● Keep to an agenda. Guard against drifting way from the main objectives.

● Lead the discussion on each item but do not dominate everyone or sit in judgement.

● Make sure the meeting reaches a satisfactory conclusion.

● Finish by summing up the main points covered at the meeting and, if appropriate, give the date of a follow-up meeting.

Remember that a successful meeting is one where everyone leaves feeling confident that they know exactly what is going to happen next and who is going to be responsible for actioning the points made.

CHECKLIST

● Have you decided whether to keep a computerised or paper diary?

● Do yo appreciate the importance of keeping your diary up to date?

● Does your reception area convey a good impression?

● Is it adequately equipped?

● Do you make sure your visitors are greeted with a warm welcome?

● Do you know how to deal with visitors who do not have an appointment?

● Could you handle an awkward visitor?

● Are you getting the best results from your meetings?

● Could you arrange a formal meeting?

● Are you familiar with the business terms used at formal meetings?

● If required, could you effectively chair a meeting?

CASE STUDIES

Dorothy creates a reception room

Dorothy, now well into her stride as far as re-vamping their antiquated office is concerned, has been given the go-ahead by Miss Porter to redesign the reception area. This is a separate office mainly used by prospective parents visiting the school.

Instead of the old and shabby furniture, Dorothy buys two comfortable couches and a smart rectangular coffee table, with an attractive tiled pattern on the top. The walls are painted in pale green, with dark green velvet curtains and a dark green carpet to add to the warm effect. There is no need for an office desk or computer equipment in the room, so Dorothy is able to achieve her aim of creating somewhere cosy and homely, in case parents have to wait some time for Miss Porter.

As finishing touches, a tropical fish tank is set up in one corner of the room, and the latest magazines are stacked neatly on the coffee table. Whenever visitors arrive, Dorothy intends to give them a welcome tea or coffee tray, complete with biscuits. Miss Porter is very pleased with the overall effect, saying that the much improved reception area will give a very good first impression of the school.

Sue computerises her diary

Having completed her computerised filing system, Sue now sets about compiling a computerised diary. On this she puts not only her appointments, but a list of every temp working for her each week and where they are working, with telephone numbers in case she needs to contact them. She also includes 'memory joggers' to help her to remember people she should be contacting each day.

Sue finds a computerised diary ideal for her ever changing needs. She updates it daily and prints herself out a copy which she puts on the wall.

Stephen rides roughshod over his team

Stephen calls an office meeting to be held after work one evening. He intends to discuss the housing market in general and the poor performance of his office in particular. He asks Margaret, one of the typists, to take the minutes.

Stephen takes the chair and the meeting lasts for one hour precisely. The precise time is achieved by Stephen looking at his watch every five minutes determined to keep to schedule.

The meeting achieves nothing. He puts everyone's backs up within the first few minutes blaming them for the office's poor performance, refusing to accept that he could having something to do with it. When the two negotiators try to put their point of view he refuses to listen.

As with most things Stephen dominates the entire meeting, giving a sermon to the rest and ignoring their protests. When the hour is up, the staff leave as quickly as they possibly can, talking about Stephen to each other on their way out. Stephen is left wondering what went wrong.

John copes with a difficult patient

A patient comes into the Outpatients Department one day asking to be seen by a consultant who is not in the hospital that day. The conversation goes like this:

John: Mr Fry, I understand you wish to see Mr Johnson?

Mr Fry: Yes I do. He did my operation three weeks ago. I went home last week, but now I feel terrible and it's his fault. I demand to see him now.

John: I'm afraid it is not possible for you to see him today. He's not here. He works at Mindley Hospital on Tuesdays.

Mr Fry: Oh yes. You're just saying that, aren't you? Just because I haven't got an appointment. Well, I want to speak to the person in charge.

John: I **am** in charge, Mr Fry, and I repeat that Mr Johnson is not here. Now if you will come into my office we will sort something out for you.

John wants to get Mr Fry away from the Outpatients hall as he is causing a scene. Reluctantly, Mr Fry follows John into his office. John makes a 'phone call to one of his receptionists.

John: Now, Mr Fry, Mr Johnson's Registrar can see you today at the end of her clinic, if that will help.

Mr Fry: Her clinic! A woman. I'm sure a woman will not be able to deal with *my* problems. This is just not good enough, you know.

John: Now, Mr Fry, I understand that you are upset, but Dr Rashid
           is extremely competent and this appointment I am offering
           you is a special one. Otherwise I can fit you in with Mr
           Johnson next week.

Mr Fry: No, I suppose she'll do, and — er — thank you for arranging
           it. I'm sorry if I seem difficult, but I'm just scared that some-
           thing has gone wrong.

John understands Mr Fry's fears, but knows that he has to be firm in
such a situation. He reassures Mr Fry, who is later seen by the Registrar
and eventually returns home feeling much happier.

POINTS FOR DISCUSSION

1. Design an ideal reception area for a small business employing just
    one receptionist. Discuss your chosen layout with a partner.

2. Do you think that 'up market' business lunches lead to increased
    business opportunities?

3. Do you consider that the formal business terms used at meetings are
    really necessary? Give the reasons for your answer.

10
A Place for Thinking and Doing

The effective management of an office relies on a good deal of 'thinking and doing'. Contrary to the opinion of many, the thinking is just as important as the doing. New ideas, making decisions, prioritising your day, all take a considerable amount of thought as well as action.

In this chapter we will discuss:

- deciding your priorities
- developing sound proposals
- brain storming
- listening to others
- asking questions
- asking for co-operation
- making and implementing decisions
- dealing with customers and suppliers
- expanding your office.

DECIDING YOUR PRIORITIES

Arranging a working day is something that many managers have trouble with. This particularly applies to those who are not prepared to delegate. For instance, if you spend half the day on the telephone chasing an order, you are not going to be able to manage your office effectively. Far better to let a member of your staff chase the order, leaving you free to carry out your managing duties.

It is very important to have a schedule to work to each day. If possible, prepare this the day before so that you know what you hope to achieve. Allocate specific times for receiving visitors, and let your staff see that, although you are technically always available to answer their queries and problems, you do also have your own job to do, so you cannot chat all day long.

Keeping a diary will obviously help you to sort out your priorities each day. Making sure you are always on top of the paperwork will help too, because then you will not feel overwhelmed by a paper mountain, and you will be able to find what you need easily, thus saving precious time.

Managing an office means making sure that your own and everyone else's time is being used in the most effective way possible. Sort out your priorities and keep to them!

DEVELOPING SOUND PROPOSALS

In order to develop sound management proposals, you will need to be a 'thinking' person. New ideas and variations on old ideas should be constantly revolving in your mind. Write down ideas and proposals as you think of them. Then look at what you have written, perhaps discussing the matter with a colleague. Think every idea and proposal through from every angle.

We all think differently according to the type of person we are. Some of us are creative, often thinking of quite unusual and sometimes outrageous ideas. A creative person will know what he or she wants to achieve and will set about realising that aim at any cost. On the other hand a more logically minded person will think ideas through from A to Z, only proceeding from stage to stage if the idea still seems feasible.

Creative people, in general, get more done. They tend to be the 'high flyers', often taking chances, somehow knowing that most times they will be successful. There is a very true saying: 'You get out of life what you put into it.' If you show a little creativity, mixed with an element of chance, when developing your proposals, you might not succeed every single time, but when you do the results will be worth the wait!

BRAIN STORMING

Brain storming is often a very effective way of solving problems at work. At a brain storming session, everyone needs to feel totally uninhibited and equal. There should be no leader. You and your staff must work together as a team.

The idea is that all those present offer their suggestions and ideas for solving the problem in question. These are written down in a haphazard fashion on a piece of paper (see figure 21). No one should offer criticism or judgement on these suggestions at this stage.

After the session has ended you can, perhaps with the aid of someone else, sort out the suggestions into some sort of logical order and look at

IDEAS

fancy dress bouncy castle
treasure hunt
sports games punch and judy
games childrens entertainment - magic show
playing cards clown show
swimming gala
playground trip to zoo
talent competition
'Belle' and 'Beau'
of Hotel competition children's party
duplo/lego drawing competition

TO TRY THIS YEAR

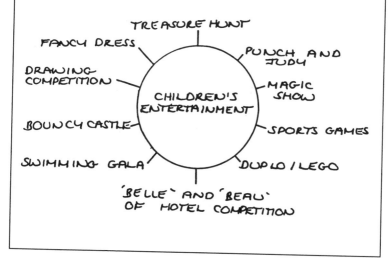

Fig. 21. A brain storming session for proposed children's entertainment at The Ship Hotel.

125

them in more detail. Any that are seen to be of immediate use should be implemented. Any others that may be of use in the future can be recorded and filed away in the appropriate place.

As well as solving problems, brain storming sessions can also be used to generate new ideas and increase creativity. Just so long as they are organised as an informal gathering, with everyone equally involved, they can be both good fun and of tremendous benefit.

LISTENING TO OTHERS

Brain storming sessions involve listening to others. In fact, many day-to-day business dealings involve listening to others. Unfortunately, however, good listeners are hard to find.

No one actually teaches us to listen, in the same way as we are taught to read and write. It is an important skill that we have to develop for ourselves. Listening to others gives us valuable information. Most of us spend as much time listening as speaking in our everyday working life. The problem is, how much of what we hear do we retain? The experts will say — not nearly enough.

It is possible to work at becoming a good listener. Here are some tips to help you:

● Make yourself interested in what is being said. The information might not seem useful now but it could be later on.

● Take notes.

● Do not interrupt until the speaker pauses, or invites you to comment.

● Help the speaker along by showing positive body language such as a nod or a smile.

● Do not pre-judge. Listen to what the speaker has to say **before** deciding whether you agree with the views being expressed.

● Try not to let your mind wander, even if you are bored.

● Finally, never fall asleep. It is very bad manners and you will definitely not remember what was said!

ASKING QUESTIONS

Asking questions forms an important part of our everyday lives. Small children ask their parents questions, almost constantly it seems, in order to extend their knowledge. Older children ask their parents and their teachers questions with the same aim in mind.

As adults questions still play a part in our lives. At work you can extract a good deal of information from others by asking **relevant** questions.

The two types of questions

Questions can be said to be 'open ended' or 'closed'. An open ended question such as 'What effect do you think the new self service store will have on our profits for this year?' calls for a fairly extensive answer. A closed question such as: 'Are you going to the canteen for lunch today?' can only usually be answered with a 'yes' or 'no'. Both have their uses according to the information you require.

The following tips should help you to ask effective questions:

● Wait for the right time to ask your question.

● Ask just one question at a time. If you ask one question and then immediately follow on with another, you will cause confusion.

● Put your question in a way that will be easily understood.

● Whenever you have to ask an awkward question be careful how you phrase it.

● Wait for an answer to your question without butting in.

● Listen carefully to the answer you are given, so that you really understand it. Make notes if necessary.

● If the answer does not satisfy you, ask another question.

● Always remember that questions should be asked for specific reasons, not just as a way of interrupting someone else.

ASKING FOR CO-OPERATION

It has been said that managers can fail because they do not think to say 'please'. Perhaps this is a little simplistic, but the way you treat your staff will certainly make a difference as far as their loyalty to you is concerned.

If you expect co-operation from your staff, you must first know what you want them to do. The next step is to speak to them in such a way that they feel they cannot refuse to help you. Make them feel they belong. Let them see that there will be something in it for them, even if that something is only a job at the end of the month because they, in their small way, will have helped to keep the organisation afloat.

There is no doubt that most people respond to the right treatment. If you show a positive attitude with a smile and a 'please would you mind doing so and so' approach, you are far more likely to get the required response, than if you say 'Go and do so and so, now!'

MAKING AND IMPLEMENTING DECISIONS

Many people find it almost impossible to make decisions, let alone implement them! Such people will not, generally speaking, make good managers.

As life is full of decisions in both our home and working life, it is a good idea to become used to them and to turn yourself into a decisive person. A decisive person gets things done. An indecisive person just thinks about getting things done.

When making an important decision:

- Assemble the facts relating to the decision to be made.

- Identify the choices available. If necessary do a 'PMI' (pluses, minuses and interesting points!).

- Assess whether anyone else needs to be involved in making the decision.

- Consider the risk factor. What will happen if the wrong decision is taken?

- Select the option with the lowest risk factor, as long as it still satisfies the aim.

- Once the decision is made, act on it as soon as you can.

- Above all, try never to make 'on the spot' or rash decisions that you might regret later on.

The decisions you make in your working life may not always turn out to be the right ones, but as long as you can learn from any mistakes, all will not have been lost. Generally speaking, even an incorrect decision is better than no decision at all.

DEALING WITH CUSTOMERS AND SUPPLIERS

Customers

It is said that 'the customer is always right'. Of course, we all know that this is not strictly true, but much of the time you have to at least pretend that it is!

Dealing with customers will often take a great deal of tact and diplomacy. You should never forget that you rely upon them totally if your organisation is to succeed. The majority of the time your everyday dealings will be quite straightforward and both the customers and you will be happy, but unfortunately this is not always the case.

Dealing with an angry customer

Whenever you have to deal with an angry customer the first thing to remember is not to allow yourself to become emotional or flustered. This will just aggravate the situation. Find out first of all why the customer is angry and whether their anger is justified. Should the mistake be on the customer's side, explain very politely what you think has happened and all should then be well. If, however, the mistake rests with you or your organisation use the following tips to deal with the situation:

● Explain to the customer what has happened and offer your sincere apologies.

● Next, try to rectify the mistake as quickly as you possibly can. Apologies are all very well, but if the matter is not sorted out, the apology will be of little use, and the customer will become even more irate — with good reason.

● Never lose your temper with a customer, even if it turns out that they were in the wrong. If the customer complains, you must always be polite, apologetic and reassuring. That way mistakes can be rectified without loss of business in the future.

Suppliers

Most offices rely on suppliers as well as customers. Suppliers will give you what you need to carry out your business and they too should be treated with respect.

If you are managing your own office it will be up to you to find suppliers who will provide you with top quality goods as well as top quality service. When your office is part of a larger organisation you will probably have to rely on central suppliers.

It is very important that you show your suppliers right from the outset that you are not prepared to tolerate any inefficiency on their part. Never complain just for the sake of it, but on the other hand, never let them take advantage of your better nature.

EXPANDING YOUR OFFICE

It is quite possible that due to increased business you will want or need to expand your office. How you go about this will depend, to some extent, on whether the office is your own or you are managing it on behalf of an organisation.

Expanding your own office

The first thing to say about expanding your office is **don't**, unless you are sure the time is right. Many small businesses survive very well until they are made bigger, with more staff, more overheads etc, and then they go under. Make sure it doesn't happen to you.

When and if you do feel that you are ready to expand, give serious thought to how you want to do it. Do you want to open another office? Do you want to employ more staff in your present office? Do you want to increase your range of products/service? All these questions should be answered and a good deal of research carried out before any expansion takes place.

Expansion usually means finding more money, and unless you already have that money, you will need to approach a bank or some other financial institution and ask them for a loan. Remember that they are unlikely to 'throw good money after bad' and will only consider you for a loan if your present business is showing signs of success. You will need to supply audited accounts and possibly a business plan too, so that they can see what you intend to do.

Do not rush into expansion. Take your time, do your research and tread very carefully.

Expanding someone else's office

If you are running an office on behalf of an organisation it is most likely that they will be involved in the expansion of your office themselves. They will have decided the time is right and you will not have that kind of responsibility to worry about, although you might well have been asked for your opinion. They, rather than you, will hold the purse strings too, so you will not have a free hand to expand just where you want to. Everything will normally be done according to company policy.

It is inevitable that expansion will mean upheaval. The biggest upheaval will probably be if the office has to be physically moved to larger premises. This may upset the staff, especially if they had been particularly attached to the old office. Also, expansion often goes hand in hand with an increase in staff. This could cause resentment amongst the 'old timers', especially if the new members of staff are seen to be treated better than their resident colleagues.

Expanding a business is exciting, but it can also be fraught with worries and problems. Keep your present staff happy, however, and you will be well on your way to a happy future.

CHECKLIST

● Do you manage your time at work effectively?

● Are you aware of your plan for the day, before the day begins?

● Are you a creative person?

● Can you see the benefits of brainstorming sessions?

● Do you listen to other people?

● Are you prepared to act on other people's ideas?

● Do you ask relevant questions and listen to the answers?

● Are you aware of the difference between open and closed questions?

● Are you able to make decisions?

● Do you implement those decisions immediately?

● Do you know how to handle customers and suppliers?

- Is your office ready for expansion?

- Have you decided how to expand?

- Are your staff aware of what is going on?

CASE STUDIES

Dorothy learns to listen

Dorothy has never been very good at listening to others. She has always had her own opinion about things and she allows others to interfere with that opinion only very occasionally.

Since Wendy's arrival, however, things are gradually changing. Dorothy enjoys listening to Wendy, particularly when they discuss the new technology, which up till now Dorothy has avoided.

Dorothy finds herself listening to Wendy more and more. Wendy has led an exciting life and her knowledge of so many things is much more extensive than Dorothy's. Dorothy realises what she has been missing all these years by not listening more to other people and resolves to be a changed person in the future.

Sue is conciliatory

Sue finds herself talking on the telephone to a very irate company director. The conversation goes like this:

'Mrs Read, hello. My name is Roger Webb, managing director of Webbs in the town. We get our temps from you.' Mr Webb sounds very cross.

'Yes, hello Mr Webb. How nice to speak to you.' Sue tries to sound unconcerned as she waits for the onslaught. 'It's about Rosie Knights, the temp you sent to cover for my secretary. She's useless. She can't even use the computer. How can I manage with a complete imbecile?' Mr Webb's voice gets higher and higher.

'I'm sorry to hear about Rosie, Mr Webb. I did explain to your secretary last week that she was not experienced in Word for Windows, but your secretary said it didn't matter and that you would show her. I'm sorry that this message did not get to you.' Sue tries to explain as best she can.

'Oh, silly Carol. I told her I wanted someone experienced. I haven't got the time or the patience to show the girl. So what will you do? She's a nice enough girl otherwise, I suppose.' Mr Webb's voice takes on more control, as if admitting that his own secretary was more to blame than Sue and the agency.

'If you can spare Rosie tomorrow, Mr Webb, I'll train her myself,' Sue offers. 'After all she is with you for three weeks so it will certainly be worth it. We normally train all our girls prior to sending them out, but Rosie has only just joined us and your secretary said on Friday it was an emergency.'

'Very well, I'll tell her to come to you tomorrow. Carol forgot about a replacement until the end of last week. There is no reason why I should take it out on Rosie, I suppose. Thank you for offering to help, Mrs Read.' Mr Webb sounds quite sheepish now, obviously regretting his outburst.

Sue has defused a difficult situation with her offer to help and everyone ends up happy.

Stephen goes from bad to worse

Stephen, continuing in his usual ham-fisted way, has given a set of rules to each of the staff. Each one begins 'You must . . . . . .'! By now all the staff are getting very fed up and are actively looking for new jobs. They are all willing and conscientious people if treated properly but Stephen's dictatorial attitude has come across to them once too often.

John brain storms with his team

John has organised a brain storming session for the new Outpatients Department. He wants the open plan office area to be a 'nice place to work in'. He asks the staff for their views on how this can be achieved. They have a very informative session with everyone taking part on equal terms and by the end John has some good ideas that he knows he will be able to incorporate in the new office design.

POINTS FOR DISCUSSION

1. With a partner or partners organise a brain storming session. See what you can come up with using the heading: 'Staff holidays — 4 weeks or 5'.

2. List six examples of open ended questions and six examples of closed questions.

3. 'Expanding your office'. List as many disadvantages as you can possibly think of.

11
Health, Safety and Security

The health and safety of workers should always come first, even if safe methods of working result in lower profits. Security plays an important part too. Confidential documents must not be left lying around. Premises need to be securely locked at night and any money, such as petty cash, should be looked after properly.

In this chapter we will discuss:

- understanding the legal requirements
- avoiding accidents
- using VDUs
- arranging first aid and fire precautions
- organising cleaning staff
- handling the petty cash
- managing visitor security.

UNDERSTANDING THE LEGAL REQUIREMENTS

Until the 1940s office workers were not protected by law in any way. Unlike their colleagues working in factories, no one seemed to think they needed any form of safeguard in so far as working conditions were concerned. The Industrial Injuries Act of 1946 provided an insurance scheme for all workers, but it was not until the Offices, Shops and Railway Premises Act of 1963 that office working conditions began to improve.

This Act laid down minimum requirements for first aid and safety, lighting, heating, washing facilities etc, as well as stating the minimum space each worker should have to work in. Unfortunately, however, this Act did not apply to all offices, schools and colleges being two notable exceptions.

In 1974 the Health and Safety at Work Act was passed and things really began to improve for office workers. This Act encompassed most of the points made in the 1963 Act but went far further, laying responsibility for health and welfare on both the employees and employers. Even more importantly it covered *all* office staff.

The Health and Safety at Work Act – employers' guide

- all **equipment** must be provided and maintained in a safe manner. This means choosing the right equipment for the job and keeping that equipment regularly serviced.

- A **safe place** of work must be provided with safe access and exit. Trailing flexes, rubbish piled up in escape routes etc, all constitute hazards.

- Safe **systems** of working should be in operation, so as to avoid unnecessary accidents.

- Adequate **facilities** should be provided for the welfare of staff. These include first aid provisions, clean toilets and somewhere to take meal breaks.

- Staff should receive **training** and instruction to enable them to use equipment and machinery properly.

- **Transporting** and handling equipment should not cause any risk to health for employees.

- Care needs to be taken when **outside contractors** are visiting the premises, to see that employees are not put at risk by work being carried out.

Responsibilities of employees

- to take care of the health and safety of themselves and anyone who should come into contact with them

- to make sure they do not interfere or misuse anything provided for the health and safety of themselves or anyone else

- to co-operate with an employer to ensure that the health and safety requirements are fulfilled.

Other workplace legislation

More recently the Management of Health and Safety At Work Regulations 1992 was brought in to make sure that the employer was fulfilling his or her obligations. The Act states that the employer should make regular inspections of the workplace to assess risk areas, and take action on those risks. Examples of risks could be trailing flexes, loose wiring, faulty equipment etc.

The Workplace Regulations 1992 were brought in at the same time. Briefly these regulations cover the provision of:

- effective maintenance of the workplace

- sufficient quantities of fresh or purified air (purified air refers to air conditioning systems)

- a comfortable working temperature. In an office this should be not less than 16 degrees centigrade. There is no upper limit!

- adequate lighting, preferably natural light

- clean places in which to work. This refers to the actual office as well as to toilets and changing facilities. Minimum toilet and washing facilities are laid down, and changing areas should be provided for both men and women

- at leat 11 cubic metres for every office worker, plus adequate space to move around, from desk to desk in an open plan office or from office to office in safety

- suitable desks and chairs for each office worker

- windows, doors etc constructed of safety materials and to be safe

- drinking water for all staff, clearly labelled. Also rest and meal facilities away from the workplace, with special facilities provided for expectant and nursing mothers.

As you will see from the above, office workers today are certainly well protected and as an office manager it is your duty to see that every one of the above criteria are adhered to at all times.

AVOIDING ACCIDENTS

As long as the regulations laid down by the various Acts are strictly followed, any accidents should be kept to an absolute minimum.

Make sure that your workers are not working too hard, so that they become tired and clumsy. If that happens what is normally a safe office environment can become an unsafe one, with workers leaving bags around, not checking machinery before use and failing to spot a hazard, all because they are too tired to notice.

It is also important to ensure that your staff are fully instructed on all safe methods of working. They cannot be expected to know about a potential hazard unless you, or someone appointed by you, has explained it to them.

Avoiding accidents is really a question of common sense and that common sense needs to be instilled by you. Never cut corners where safety is concerned, and always remain mindful of the regulations under which you operate.

USING VDUs

For many years now allegations have been made that the continual use of VDUs (Visual Display Units) can cause health problems. These problems are said to include:

- deterioration of eyesight
- epilepsy
- headaches
- stress
- radiation risk to unborn babies
- repetitive strain injury (RSI).

A great deal of research has been made into all these allegations and it is not thought that the VDU itself poses any risk at all to our health. What is important, however, is the way that we use the VDU. If we sit in one position all day, use an unsuitable chair or workstation/desk, and do not have adequate lighting, then we are likely to suffer from a health problem.

Largely to address these health worries, in 1993 legislation was introduced known as the Health and Safety (Display Screen Equipment) Regulations. The main aim of these regulations is to make sure that 'frequent users' (over one hour a day continuously) are sitting in a proper position, do not have to strain to read the screen and are given regular breaks. The regulations also say that an employee is entitled to ask the employer to pay for an eye test, and if it is proven that glasses are necessary because of VDU use, then the employer will be expected to pay for the glasses too.

ARRANGING FIRST AID AND FIRE PRECAUTIONS

First aid

Under the Health and Safety At Work Act every employer should provide first aid for employees. This includes treatment for minor injuries and also emergency treatment necessary to keep a person alive until an ambulance arrives.

All offices should contain a first aid kit including plasters, bandages, eye pads and dressings. It is also a good idea to include a first aid book in the kit.

Even a small office should contain someone who is trained in basic first aid, and it is up to you to arrange for a member of your staff to attend a first aid course. Volunteers for first aid are usually in plentiful supply. Television drama seems to have generated what could be said to be a morbid interest in health matters!

Fire precautions

Fire can spread extremely rapidly. You and your staff need to know exactly what to do if a fire does break out in your office. All offices should contain a fire extinguisher, of the correct type (your local Fire Officer will advise you), and this fire extinguisher needs to be regularly serviced. Make sure that you and your staff know how to use it in order to take action before the fire brigade arrive.

You also need to instruct everyone on evacuation procedures, and if your office is not easy to ge out of, regular fire drills will standardise this procedure and make it easy to put into action should a real emergency arise.

ORGANISING CLEANING STAFF

The staff who clean your office may be employed directly by you, by your organisation, or by a cleaning contract company.

When you are responsible for your own cleaners, it is very important to tell them exactly what you want cleaned and to provide them with sufficient high quality products to carry out that cleaning. It is also important to treat your cleaners decently and not as members of an inferior society as some managers are prone to do.

Most cleaning is carried out either early in the morning or in the evening. Your cleaners will need a key to the office and they will have to be responsible enough to see that the office is locked when they leave. Do not leave confidential paper lying about. Even the most reliable and loyal cleaners will be hard pushed to ignore a confidential document that makes for very interesting reading!

If at any time you feel the cleaning is not up to standard they say so. Be polite but firm and make it clear that you expect more effort to be made in the future. Conversely, if your cleaners do an excellent job then reward them occasionally with a box of chocolates or a bottle of wine. A little appreciation goes a long way!

HANDLING THE PETTY CASH

The word 'petty' in this context means 'small'. Therefore petty cash refers to small amounts of cash kept in the office. This cash can be used for:

- coffee, tea, sugar, juice etc
- postage stamps
- window cleaning
- cleaning materials
- emergency stationery items
- flowers and small presents
- taxi or bus fares.

Petty cash should be stored in a locked cash box and this box should preferably live in a lockable drawer or cupboard. Any cash taken from the box needs to be accounted for on a petty cash voucher. Cash removed without a note will disappear without trace and can cause bad feeling in the office if someone is accused of taking it.

Take care not to keep too big a 'float' at any one time. Should the office be burgled, locked cash boxes will be one of the first items to go.

MANAGING VISITOR SECURITY

Most people today are fully aware of the need for good security at work.

In certain organisations where top secret or highly confidential documents are housed, even more than the normal amount of vigilance is necessary.

It is important to keep a record of visitors' arrivals and departures even in the smallest of offices, so that should a theft or a breach of confidentiality occur, it will show at a glance who was on the premises at the time. In a small office a note might be made in the diary. Larger organisations often have a visitors book, usually kept in the reception area, giving details of who visits, where they came from, who they came to see and the time of their arrival and departure. Visitors could also be issued with a badge saying 'visitor' so that everyone knows they are not a member of the regular workforce.

It goes without saying that confidential papers and files should be kept out of the way of visitors. For instance, someone waiting in your office for you to arrive could easily lean over your desk and read confidential material that you have been careless enough to leave out. Don't let this happen. Apart from anything else, this material could contain details of what the two of you had planned to discuss and it could affect the visitor's judgement before discussions begin.

Many organisations tend to be rather lax about security and this is a big mistake. A breach of security causes problems for everyone concerned, and can lead to a feeling of mistrust which is hard to shake off.

CHECKLIST

● Are you aware of the legislation covering office workers?

● Does your office comply with these regulations?

● If not, what do you intend to do about it?

● Do you take adequate precautions to avoid accidents in your office?

● Are you aware of the special regulations regarding VDU operation?

● Do your desks, chairs and working environment provide a safe place for your VDU operators to work?

● Are your staff aware of first aid and fire precautions?

● Are your cleaners treated well?

● Do they do a good job and is your office always clean?

● Do you take good care of your petty cash?

● Are you aware of the need to log the arrival and departure of visitors to your office?

● Do you keep confidential papers well out of the way of your visitors?

CASE STUDIES

Dorothy trips up

Dorothy trips over in the office one day. The wires leading to all the new equipment they have purchased trail across the floor and the accident was inevitable. Dorothy is given adequate first aid by one of the teachers, but is till in considerable pain and is sent home.

After a week off with a sprained ankle Dorothy goes to see Miss Porter to tell her that she feels the office is just too cramped for them now that they have increased the amount of machinery being used, and that it is dangerous too, due to all the trailing flexes. Miss Porter agrees to think about a more suitable place for their office to be sited.

Sue changes her cleaner

Sue's cleaner has not been doing a very good job of late. Because of an increase in workload, Sue has found it necessary to take over another room in their house for office purposes. The cleaner says that she cannot be expected to clean three rooms properly in the same time as it took to clean just two. Sue realises that she has a point and agrees to increase her hours and wages.

Another month goes by and things do not improve. In the end Sue is forced to look for a replacement cleaner. A dirty office means not only an unhealthy working environment, but it also gives a bad impression to clients and employees who call in to see her.

Stephen mishandles the petty cash

Stephen has a problem with the petty cash. At the end of the month it doesn't balance. He blames this on everyone but himself. Margaret has actually seen Stephen take money out of the cash box for stamps without putting in a voucher. She asks him, very politely, if this could possibly explain the discrepancy. Stephen denies all knowledge of the inci-

dent and rants and raves for days over the missing £2.00. This just adds
to the bad feeling already present amongst his staff.

John goes by the book

John's office move is coming closer. He has been spending a considerable time looking around the new building as he wants it to be not only
attractive to look at, but also comfortable and safe to work in.

John reads up on all the relevant legislation concerning health and
safety to acquaint himself with the requirements. He is particularly concerned about VDU use and he makes sure that suitable desks and chairs
are being purchased for the relevant members of staff to use. He also
sends all the VDU operators off for an eye check and arranges for the
Trust to pay for glasses where they are considered necessary.

POINTS FOR DISCUSSION

1. Do you think office workers today are well enough protected by
    legislation concerning their health and welfare? Give reasons for
    your answer.

2. Make a list of all the possible hazards you can think of that could
    cause an accident in an office.

3. You work in a small office on the third floor of a building. What
    would you need to do to ensure that if a fire broke out you and your
    staff would be able to cope?

12
Coping With an Office Move

Organising a successful office move is rather like a military operation. Absolutely every stage needs to be thoroughly planned in advance if you are to avoid last minute disasters.

In this chapter we will discuss:

- planning staff changes
- arranging removals
- planning ahead
- getting the new office ready
- notifying customers and suppliers
- packing up
- surviving moving day
- settling in.

PLANNING STAFF CHANGES

An office move can, of course, be either short or long distance. If the move is long distance then staff will need to be told well in advance, and if they are willing to move with the office, they should, if at all possible, be offered employment in your new location.

On the other hand, should they be unable or unwilling to uproot themselves and their families then, depending upon the terms of their contract of employment, they will be either made redundant or given notice. (For instance, if a contract signed by the employee states that the person must be willing to work in any part of the country, and when it comes to it that person refuses, they will not, strictly speaking be entitled to redundancy pay.)

The third possibility is that you will no longer have a job to offer certain people in your new location. Should that be the case then those people will normally be entitled to redundancy payments.

A move to new office premises in the same area usually means the

143

same personnel being employed, although there could be fluctuations in staffing levels. For instance, a move to larger premises will probably mean an increase in staff, whereas a move to smaller premises because of a downturn in business could mean fewer jobs available.

Whatever the changes to your staff try to make time to speak to everyone personally explaining the position and offering all the help and advice that you possibly can. An office move can seem just as traumatic to many people as a house move. They may be very attached to their own 'space' and belongings. Try to understand any hesitancy on their part, especially if you yourself feel very excited and enthusiastic about what lies ahead.

ARRANGING REMOVALS

There are specialised removal companies for office moves. It is certainly worth while obtaining a quotation from at least one such company, as they are definitely the experts and are unlikely to moan about dragging the furniture up four flights of stairs to your new premises. Unfortunately, however, these specialised companies often charge a lot more than the smaller general removal people, so unless your organisation is paying for the move you would be just as well to obtain other quotes too.

Removal quotes cost nothing, and every company will offer you a slightly different type of service. Walk round with each estimator who comes to see you, checking on exactly what that company will offer you. Compare quotations carefully. Check for adequate insurance cover and whether the quote includes packing the office items or if you have to do this yourself. Ask how they intend to transport the computers and other especially fragile equipment.

Do not necessarily accept the cheapest quote. On the other hand the most expensive company will not necessarily be the best. You should weigh up the pros and cons carefully before making your decision and do not pay anything more than a deposit in advance — just in case they do not do the job to your satisfaction.

PLANNING AHEAD

Some of us thrive on lists. Shopping lists, jobs to do lists, telephone call lists, letters to write lists. Lists for everything. When moving your office, those of you who are 'list orientated' will find life much easier than those who try to remember everything without writing it down.

Here are some of the lists you could make:

● a list for each member of staff involved, giving his or her duties during the move

● a list for packing

● a list of people to contact by telephone or fax to advise them of the move

● a list of what needs to be done to your new office premises prior to moving in

● a list of people to write to advising them of the move

● a list of what to do on moving day

● a list of priorities after moving day.

Of course, it is perfectly feasible to put all your lists onto computer disk, especially the lists for each member of staff. This is perhaps one of the times, however, when it could be easier to jot your own lists down on pieces of paper so that you can carry them around with you at all times.

As we said at the beginning of this chapter, planning in advance is crucial for a successful office move. Not only have you got to plan the move itself but it is also important to make sure that no routine office matters are going to have to be dealt with on the actual moving day. Urgent matters will just have to be handled if and when they arise, but they are less likely to arise if you have planned well ahead.

An example of a list or programme for the actual moving day is shown in figure 22.

GETTING THE NEW OFFICE READY

In an ideal world you will have had possession of your new office before actually moving in. This will enable you to do any necessary decorating and rearranging ready for the furniture and equipment to be brought straight in on moving day. Assuming this to be the case, spend some time deciding how you want your office to look both in terms of decoration and layout. If you can afford to re-carpet and re-decorate and the

MOVING DAY

0800 hrs	Arrive at office. Pack up last minute items.
0900 hrs	Other workers arrive. Give them their last minute instructions.
1000 hrs	Removers arrive.
1200 hrs	Go to new office. Check electricity and telephone supply.
1300 hrs	Go to local sandwich shop and buy lunch for everyone.
1500 hrs	Begin to arrange office furniture and link up machines.
1700 hrs	Unpack urgent items.
1830 hrs	Go home — exhausted!

Remember to makes lots of tea and coffee for everyone at regular intervals, particularly the removal men. Remember to tip them before they leave.

Fig. 22. Schedule for moving day.

office needs it, then do so. The more impressive your office looks the more comfortable everyone will feel about working in it, particularly if your office move has met with some resistance from other staff.

If you are not able to gain access to your office prior to moving day, then you will have to do the best you can. Do not start repainting the walls at 0900 hrs, hoping to get it finished by the time the furniture arrives at midday. Any re-decoration will just have to wait until later on. Unfortunately this will probably mean taking out much of what you have moved in, or at least moving it all around, but that cannot be avoided.

Unless you have been able to plan and decorate your office prior to moving in do not rush into anything. Live with the office as it is for a while until you know definitely what you want to do to improve it.

NOTIFYING CUSTOMERS AND SUPPLIERS

Part of your planning ahead should include notifying all your customers and suppliers of your office move. Send out letters in plenty of time stating when you are moving and where you are moving to. If there are days when the office will be closed altogether then say so.

The Post Office offer a mail redirection service which you should arrange with them. This will take care of any stray mail from people you would not normally be in contact with. An advertisement in the local paper could help too, particularly if you are in a service industry where people can walk in at any time. Someone who had made a special journey to come and see you might feel a little peeved to find you gone to an address some miles away. Employment agencies, for example, have people constantly visiting their offices without an appointment. Advertising would tell those people of an impending office move.

PACKING UP

Many removal companies will come and pack everything up for you. Unless you are on a limited budget this could be a very good idea, especially if your office has to function normally before, during and after the move.

Many of us, however, either cannot afford the packing facilities or do not trust anyone other than ourselves to do the packing. Should you be in this position, make sure you leave yourself plenty of time to pack everything up very carefully. Pack infrequently used items first, well in advance, and then work out a packing schedule to take you up to the actual moving day. Label all boxes very clearly. Otherwise you will end up in an awful mess at the other end trying to sort everything out.

With an office move there are likely to be certain items that are used all the time. These will just have to be packed on moving day. Very fragile or important items could perhaps be carried in your own car rather than in the removal van.

A methodical approach to packing will ensure that it is correctly done without any major hassles or breakages.

SURVIVING MOVING DAY

Moving house is said to be one of the most stressful things we do in life. Moving office is not usually quite so stressful, but if you allow yourself to become worked up you could well feel extremely 'stressed out' by the end of the day.

To begin with, make sure you have a good breakfast to set you up for the day ahead. After all, there is no guarantee of when you will get some lunch! Next arrive at the office early to enable you to pack up all the last minute bits and pieces. When your staff arrive make sure they all know what they are going to do for the day.

Once the removal men arrive you should be in charge of directing operations. Try to keep calm when they drop your favourite potted plant or scratch a desk manoeuvring it down the steep stairs. Hopefully any damage will be kept to an absolute minimum, and your insurance cover will take care of anything serious. Remember that it is not your treasured home possessions that are being moved. Unless you are very attached to your office, the things being moved should not have quite the same significance!

Make sure that tea and coffee is supplied to everybody at regular intervals. Put a member of staff who is particularly prone to flap in a crisis on that job.

Above all, be nice to everyone. Go around with a smile on your face, reassuring the removal men and your staff that everything will be just fine and that the day will pass without a hitch, even if you think precisely the opposite!

As soon as the removers have loaded everything onto the lorry you will need to get to your new office ready for their arrival. If the office is moving from one part of the country to another then the furniture and equipment may not be delivered until the following day, but otherwise everything is usually offloaded the same day. Leave someone at the old office to clean everything up and to check that nothing has been left.

When directing operations in your new abode, try to have a mental or actual plan of where you want everything to go. Desks and workstations are heavy items. The removal men will not want to shift each desk into several different positions while you make up your mind where you like them best! If necessary, you can change things around later, but your priority should be to see everything in as quickly and efficiently as possible.

Remember to give the men a tip when they have finished unloading. The size of this tip will depend on the job they have done, but removers traditionally earn very low wages and £5.00 each will probably be very well received.

SETTLING IN

The day after your office move you will probably look around you and think that you will never get everything straight again. Your staff will, no doubt, feel the same way. The secret is to take one step at a time. Unpack the essentials first. Put someone in charge of answering the telephone for everyone for a couple of days; give someone else the job of dealing with everyday matters as and when they arise. Keep the normal office activity as low as you possibly can until you are organised.

Most of your customers and suppliers are likely to be sympathetic to your circumstances at least for the first few days. There are bound to be the odd one or two who insist that they are dealt with immediately, but that is why you will have asked someone to cover that for you. The business does still have to run though, even if you can't find the printer cables to link up the computer printer, or the telephones that you were sure you packed in box no 10!

All you can do is your best. Get sorted out as quickly as you feasibly can, but, once more, make sure you work methodically. Do not start any re-decoration until everything is up and running once again.

In the event of your office move being to a completely different part of the country it is very likely that you will have been forced to move house. Organising an office and house move at the same time can prove to be very demanding and stressful. If you are faced with both, then as soon as your office is operational devote as much time as you can to sorting out your new home and any family problems caused by the upheaval.

An office move can be relatively stress-free, exciting and mark the start of a new era in your working life. Planning well ahead, as well as keeping your temper, your sense of humour and your sanity throughout, will set you off on the positive road to success.

CHECKLIST

● Have you told your staff about the office move?

● Have you considered the changes the move could mean for them?

● Have you asked for several removal quotations?

● Have you made the appropriate lists and planned well in advance?

● Have you set aside some time for getting the new office ready if you are able to do so?

● Have you notified customers and suppliers of the move?

● Have you put an advertisement in the local paper advising of your new address?

● Have you prepared yourself mentally and physically for moving day?

- Have you made up your mind not to panic or lose your temper should anything go wrong?

- Have you decided to take time to settle in?

- Have you achieved what you set out to achieve at the end of the move?

CASE STUDIES

Dorothy's outlook changes

Miss Porter has thought about Dorothy's complaint about the lack of space in their office. The reception office has recently been decorated and looks very smart and Miss Porter is perfectly satisfied with her own office too. What she decides to do is to give Dorothy the present office for her own use and open up an adjoining room as an office for the two part-timers. Everyone is very pleased about this, especially since the offices adjoin to the extent that they will still be able to get together for their little chats. The move only involves shifting two desks, chairs, computers and printers next door and giving the new office a quick coat of paint.

Dorothy looks back over the last couple of years and realises just how much her outlook has changed. She feels she is now a truly up-to-date office manager ready for any challenges that might lie ahead.

Sue prospers

Although she knows she mustn't complain, Sue's business has grown to such an extent that she feels she should move into offices in the town. She looks round for suitable premises and finds a four-room office suite on the second floor of a purpose built building. Parking is available right outside and the set-up appears to be ideal.

Sue's husband knows a friend with a van and as the offices are empty they are able to move everything in gradually. She employs a painter and decorator to spruce up the offices and arranges for a new carpet to be laid throughout. By the time she has finished she is very pleased with the results.

Because of the nature of her business, Sue advertises the move in the local newspaper as well as notifying all her temps and clients. In no time at all everything is ready, and Sue is pleased that she made the decision as it gives them much more space at home once more. Her business continues to grow and she is eventually able to employ a full-time manager herself, so that she can take a back seat and enjoy her new found prosperity!

Stephen gets his comeuppance

Stephen moves offices too, but on his own! His head office has received so many complaints from the staff working with him that they tell him he is moving back to London to take on a more junior position once more. He has failed in nearly every aspect of management. His staff are delighted to get rid of him, and his replacement, who is a lady in her early 30s, proves to them that it was Stephen and not they who were at fault. They get on with the new manager really well and business quickly shows an upward trend which continues until the office is forced to expand. Ironically this is what Stephen wanted to happen, but he went about it in completely the wrong way.

John gets it right again

At last John's eagerly awaited move actually happens. The new building looks marvellous and he and all the staff are very excited. He has planned everything so well in advance that everyone knows what they are doing and the move goes very smoothly. Clinics are only disrupted for two days which is a miracle considering the enormity of the task of moving so much in such a short time.

The new Outpatients Department meets with the approval of staff and patients alike. John becomes the most respected manager in the entire hospital. He enjoys his job and his staff enjoy working with him. He seems to have found the perfect winning formula.

POINTS FOR DISCUSSION

1. How prepared do you think staff should be to move from one part of the country to another in order to safeguard their job?

2. How would you attempt to entice an important member of your staff to move to another area if he or she was not keen on the idea? What incentives do you think you could offer?

3. Assuming that it was necessary for you to move from an up-market office in one street to a rather poky office around the corner for financial reasons, how would you explain this to your customers and suppliers?

Appendix 1: National Vocational Qualifications

National Vocational Qualifications (NVQs) have been recently introduced by the National Council for Vocational Qualifications. They are available in many different subjects. Those intended to help office workers are Administration Levels 1, 2 and 3. The criteria for these NVQs were revised in 1994.

Conventional examinations aim to test your formal skill and knowledge in one or more particular subjects. NVQs are designed to prove that you can put your exam success to good use in the workplace. They deal with the practical aspects of your work.

NVQs are made up of different units. Certificates can be awarded for just one or more units, if you do not want to go on and take the full certificate.

Many of the topics listed below are included in the text of this book. If some of the words used here are unfamiliar to you, check in the Glossary for their meaning.

ADMINISTRATION LEVEL 1

Unit 1: Contribute to the efficiency of the work flow
Element 1.1   Organise own work
Element 1.2   Develop self to improve performance
Element 1.3   Maintain own work area to assist work flow

Unit 2: Contribute to the health, safety and security of the workplace
Element 2.1   Contribute to the prevention of hazards in the workplace
Element 2.2   Contribute to the limitation of damage to persons or property in the event of an accident or emergency
Element 2.3   Contribute to maintaining the security of the workplace and its contents

Unit 3: Operate and take care of equipment
Element 3.1   Follow instructions and operate equipment
Element 3.2   Keep equipment in a clean and working condition

Unit 4: Develop effective working relationships
Element 4.1   Create and maintain effective working relationships
              with other members of staff
Element 4.2   Greet and assist visitors

Unit 5: Process information
Element 5.1   Process incoming and outgoing telecommunications
Element 5.2   Supply information to meet specified requests
Element 5.3   Check and process routine, numerical information

Unit 6: Store and retrieve information using an established storage system
Element 6.1   Store information using an established storage system
Element 6.2   Obtain information from an established storage system

Unit 7: Produce text following instructions
Element 7.1   Produce text using a keyboard
Element 7.2   Produce copies using reprographic equipment

Unit 8: Handling mail
Element 8.1   Receive, sort and distribute mail
Element 8.2   Dispatch mail

Unit 9: Monitor and issue stock items
Element 9.1   Monitor and request stock
Element 9.2   Issue stock items on request

You are only awarded the full NVQ if you achieve all 9 Units. If you achieve fewer than 9, you may, however, claim a Certificate of Unit Credit for each Unit you complete.

ADMINISTRATION LEVEL 2

At Level 2 there are 8 mandatory Units and 7 optional Units. You will only be awarded the NVQ if you achieve all the mandatory Units and at least 1 of the optional Units. In addition, if you achieve the full NVQ and then complete extra optional Units, these will also be certificated. If you achieve fewer than 9 Units you will receive a Certificate of Unit Credit for each Unit that you do complete.

Mandatory Units
Unit 1: Develop self to improve performance
Element 1.1   Identify and agree own development needs
Element 1.2   Prepare and agree a plan of action to develop self
Element 1.3   Implement and review a personal development plan

Unit 2: Monitor and maintain a healthy, safe and secure workplace
Element 2.1   Monitor and maintain health and safety within the workplace
Element 2.2   Monitor and maintain the security of the workplace

Unit 3: Contribute to the effectiveness of the work flow
Element 3.1   Plan and organise own work schedule
Element 3.2   Obtain and organise information in support of own work activities
Element 3.3   Obtain and maintain physical resources to carry out own work

Unit 4: Create and maintain effective working relationships
Element 4.1   Establish and maintain working relationships with other members of staff
Element 4.2   Receive and assist visitors

Unit 5: Store, retrieve and supply information
Element 5.1   Maintain an established storage system
Element 5.2   Supply information for a specific purpose

Unit 6: Maintain data in a computer system
Element 6.1   Input data and text into a computer system
Element 6.2   Locate and retrieve data from a computer system
Element 6.3   Print documents using a computer system

Unit 7: Prepare documents
Element 7.1   Respond to correspondence
Element 7.2   Prepare a variety of documents

Unit 8: Receive and transmit information
Element 8.1   Receive and transmit information electronically
Element 8.2   Receive and send mail

Unit 9: Maintain and issue stock items
Element 9.1   Order, monitor and maintain stock
Element 9.2   Issue stock items on request

Optional Units
Unit 10: Process documents relating to goods and services
Element 10.1 Order goods and services
Element 10.2 Process claims for payment

Unit 11: Organise travel and accommodation arrangements
Element 11.1 Arrange travel for persons
Element 11.2 Book accommodation for a specified purpose

Unit 12: Contribute to the arrangement of events
Element 12.1 Assist in arrangements for the provision of supporting facilities and materials at events
Element 12.2 Assist in arrangements for the attendance of persons at events
Element 12.3 Assist in arrangements for the provision of catering services at events

Unit 13: Produce and present business documents from provided material
Element 13.1 Produce business documents from provided material using a keyboard
Element 13.2 Present business documents in a variety of formats using a keyboard

Unit 14: Produce and present business documents from recorded material
Element 14.1 Produce business documents from recorded instructions using a keyboard
Element 14.2 Present business documents in a variety of formats using a keyboard

Unit 15: Produce and present business documents from dictated material
Element 15.1 Produce business documents from dictated information using a keyboard
Element 15.2 Present business documents in a variety of formats using a keyboard

Glossary

Absent card Card used to show a file has been removed from the filing system.

Answerphone A device capable of recording telephone messages when no one is available to take them personally.

Appraisal Review of an employee's accomplishments.

Attitude The way we think or behave.

Communicate To give, receive or exchange information with others.

Curriculum Vitae (CV) meaning 'the course of a life'.

Customer Person or organisation buying goods or services.

Decision To come to a conclusion.

Delegate To give a task to another person.

Disk Storage medium used by many computers. Can be 'floppy' or 'hard'.

Draft The first, rough copy of a document.

Environment Surroundings we live and work in.

Hard copy Printout on paper.

Income Tax Tax payable to the State via the Inland Revenue on money earned.

Inland Revenue Body responsible for the administration of our tax laws, including the collection of income tax.

Interest Amount paid on a sum of money borrowed or invested in a bank or building society account.

Interpret Explain the meaning of something.

Interview Formal conversation between two or more people with a specific aim in mind.

Legislation Laws that have been made by parliament.

Memo A note used to pass information between colleagues in the same organisation.

National Insurance A scheme run by the Government to provide payment to individuals when they are sick or unemployed, as well as the state pension. It is funded with contributions made by employees as a percentage of their income and also with contributions by employers.

Profit A company's earnings after all costs have been deducted.

Program Instructions written to make a computer obey certain commands.

Recipient A person who receives something.

Recorded delivery A Royal Mail service whereby letters and packets are sent with a certificate of posting as proof that they have been posted. A signature is obtained on delivery. This service is not suitable for valuables.

Registered post A Royal Mail service, guaranteeing next day delivery to most UK destinations. A signature is collected on delivery and items of value can be sent.

Running costs Operating expenses of a business.

Targets Achievements to be gained in a specific period of time.

Telesales A method of selling by using the telephone.

Teleworking Working from home using electronic means.

Transmit To send or pass on.

Under-achieving Not reaching the required standard.

Further Reading

Brits at Work, John Mole (Nicholas Brealey Publishing).

Collins Office Handbook, Louise Bostock (HarperCollins).

The Creative Manager, Roger Evans, Peter Russell (Unwin Paperbacks).

How to Communicate at Work, Ann Dobson (How To Books Ltd).

How to Conduct Staff Appraisals, Nigel Hunt (How To Books Ltd).

How to Employ and Manage Staff, Wendy Wyatt (How To Books Ltd).

How to Manage Computers at Work, Graham Jones (How To Books Ltd).

How to Manage People at Work, John Humphries (How To Books Ltd).

How to Master Business English, Michael Bennie (How To Books Ltd).

How to Master Public Speaking, Ann Nicholls (How To Books Ltd).

How to Return to Work, Ann Dobson (How To Books Ltd).

How to Take Minutes of Meetings, Jennie Hawthorne (Kogan Page).

How to Work in an Office, Sheila Payne (How To Books Ltd).

How to Write Business Letters, Ann Dobson (How To Books Ltd).

How to Write a Report, John Bowden (How To Books Ltd).

The Manager's Guide to Solving Personnel Issues, Isobel Emanuel (Pitman).

Managing Difficult Staff, Helga Drummond (Kogan Page).

Office Procedures, Geoffrey Whitehead (Made Simple Books).

Perfect Recruitment, Dave Oates and Viv Shackleton (Arrow Business Books).

Secretarial Procedures in the Electronic Office, Desmond W Evans (Pitman).

Successful Meetings in a Week, John and Shirley Payne (Hodder and Stoughton).

Working From Home, Christopher Temple (Maddison Square).

Useful Contacts

Confederation of British Industry, Centre Point, New Oxford Street, London WC1A 1DU.

Data Protection Registrar, Wycliffe House, Water Lane, Wilmslow, Cheshire SK9 5AF.

Department of Employment, Caxton House, Tothill Street, London SW1H 9NF.

Health and Safety Executive, Information Centre, Broad Lane, Sheffield S3 7HQ.

Her Majesty's Stationery Office, PO Box 276, London SW8 5DT.

Institute of Directors, 116 Pall Mall, London SW1Y 5ED.

Institute of Management, Management House, Cottingham Road, Corby, Northants NN17 1TT.

Institute of Personnel and Development, IPM House, Camp Road, London SW19 4UX.

National Council for Vocational Qualifications, 222 Euston Road, London NW1 2BZ.

Rural Development Commission, 141 Castle Street, Salisbury, Wilts SP1 3TP.

Small Firms Information Service, Ebury Bridge House, 2 Ebury Bridge Road, London SW1 8QD.

The Information Bureau, 51 Battersea Business Centre, 103 Lavender Hill, London SW11 5QL.

The Registrar of Companies (Search Room), Companies House, 55-71 City Road, London EC1Y 1BB.

Women Returner's Network, 8 John Adam Street, London WC2N 6EZ.
Plus:

Your local Council Offices, particularly the Planning Department if setting up a new office.

Citizens Advice Bureaux

Local libraries

Banks, many of whom have extensive business information.

Index